# Workers Against the Gulag

# Workers Against the Gulag

## The New Opposition in the Soviet Union

Edited and introduced by
**Viktor Haynes** and **Olga Semyonova**

Pluto Press

First published 1979
by Pluto Press Limited
    Unit 10 Spencer Court, 7 Chalcot Road,
    London NW1 8LH
Copyright © Pluto Press 1979
    ISBN 0 86104 072 4

Cover designed by David King
Cover picture: Alexander Podrabinek being arrested
by plain-clothes men in Moscow, April 1977
Copyright Peter Reddaway, reproduced with permission
Typeset by Red Lion Setters,
    Holborn, London

Reproduced, printed and bound in Great Britain by
Cox & Wyman Ltd
London, Reading and Fakenham

# Contents

# Glossary

### The KGB and MVD:
Since Stalin's death the Soviet security services have been divided into the KGB (Committee of State Security) and MVD (Ministry of Internal Affairs). The MVD is responsible for the criminal police and controls the Internal Troops. The KGB, as the political police proper, is responsible for secret intelligence, counter-espionage and internal security. It controls the Border Guards.

### Nationalities and the Structure of the USSR:
The Soviet Union is a patchwork of different nationalities. Geographers and philologists have identified nearly 200 distinct languages and peoples within its borders. In 1970 Great Russians were 129 million out of a total population of nearly 242 million. The constitutional structure of the USSR is federal. It is composed of 15 Union Republics, each of which has the legal right to secede from the Soviet Union. Some in turn include Autonomous Republics (of which there are 22), Autonomous Regions (eight) and National Areas (ten). By far the biggest Union Republic is the Russian Socialist Federated Soviet Republic (RSFSR), which stretches right across the USSR and embraces 16 Autonomous Republics, five Autonomous Regions and 10 National Areas.

### The Procurator's Office:
The Procurator-General of the USSR and the procurators subordinate to him are responsible for ensuring that state agencies, public organisations and private citizens observe the law and for prosecuting breaches of the law. The Procurator-General is appointed by, and responsible to, the Supreme Soviet of the USSR and is, in theory, independent of the Council of Ministers and the KGB. According to article 58 of the Constitution, 'citizens of the USSR have the right to lodge a complaint against the actions of officials, state bodies and public bodies'. These complaints are addressed to the Procurator's Office.

### Samizdat:
Literally 'self-print' — the literature secretly produced and distributed by Soviet dissidents.

# Preface

There is not, nor can there ever be, absolute freedom. Nevertheless, it is important to recognise that there are certain basic human rights which ought not to be violated.

Yet these rights are being trampled upon in many parts of the world under different economic and social regimes. Socialists and communists are imprisoned in countries like Argentina, Chile, Iran, and South Africa, while non-communists are killed in Cambodia and gaoled in other communist countries.

The rulers in the Soviet Union are not concerned with political labels like 'left' and 'right' — anyone who opposes or queries the existing regime is likely to be sent to prison or incarcerated in a psychiatric hospital.

When it comes to civil and human rights, therefore, it is important that socialists should not be seen to have double standards. The British left have always been the champions of free speech, free association, free trade unions, free elections, free parliaments, in countries like Chile, Argentina, Brazil and South Africa, as well as at home. We must stand up equally for human rights in the so-called socialist countries.

If oppression takes place in the name of socialism, then socialism itself is besmirched, and those who would otherwise be in favour of a socialist society turn away in disgust. This has already happened on a vast scale, and the oppression in the Soviet Union and other 'socialist' countries has done untold harm to the cause of socialism.

Democracy and freedom have always been the instruments of genuine socialism, not its enemies. Once anti-democratic methods are used, then socialism goes out of the window. Shortly before her death at the hands of the German right in 1919, Rosa Luxemburg warned the Bolsheviks:

*'Freedom for the supporters of the Government only, for the*

1

*members of one party only — no matter how big its membership may be — is no freedom at all. Freedom is always for the man who thinks differently. This contention does not spring from a fanatical line of abstract justice, but from the fact that everything which is enlightening, healthy and purifying in political freedom derives from its independent character, and from the fact that freedom loses all its virtues when it becomes a privilege.'*

Luxemburg argued that the dictatorship of the proletariat 'would be an extension of democracy':

*'This dictatorship consists in a particular application of democracy, not in its abolition; it implies energetic action against the acquired rights and general economic relations of bourgeois society, and without this intervention a socialist transformation of society is impossible.'*

In the so-called German Democratic Republic today, it is the dictatorship of the party, not the dictatorship of the proletariat that prevails. This is underlined by the fate of Rudolf Bahro, sentenced to eight years' imprisonment for publishing in the west a marxist critique of 'real existing socialism', *The Alternative.*

This type of bureaucratic society has nothing in common with socialism, the essence of which is freedom and democracy. Socialism means the flowering of the human spirit, not its curtailment or destruction. The very idea of putting a writer, poet or scientist in prison or in a mental institution for their beliefs fills genuine socialists with horror.

It is this that turns Soviet dissidents into 'counter-revolutionaries' once they gain their freedom and reach the west. They were not always reactionaries. But they have been in labour camps, prisons, or mental hospitals merely for expressing their views, or sometimes just for demanding the implementation of the law. The west, with its apparent freedom of speech and politics, seems to them like paradise.

Roy Medvedev, a Soviet dissident who has remained a marxist and a socialist writes:

*'Socialist democracy is simultaneously a goal and a means. Democracy is essential as a value in itself. To be able to express one's thoughts and convictions freely without fear of persecution or repression is a vital aspect of a free socialist way of life. Without freedom to receive and impart information, without freedom of movement and residence, without freedom of creativity in science*

*and the arts, and without many other democratic freedoms, a true socialist society is impossible. Democracy — with all government activity open to public scrutiny — is also necessary as a means of ridding our society of bureaucracy and corruption. It offers firm protection against a relapse into arbitrary lawlessness.'*

Socialism and democracy are, therefore, synonymous. It is important to stress this because today in Britain the Conservative Party is trying to prove that left-wing socialists want an East European-style state. These same Tories who make such a song-and-dance about Soviet repression are quite happy to remain silent about what goes on in countries like Chile, Iran and South Africa.

But the fact that many Tories have double standards on the question of human rights is no reason for socialists to follow their example. Oppression is oppression, and when it is carried out in the name of socialism, then it is absolutely vital that socialists should not only protest and attack it, but also shout from the roof-tops that such oppression has nothing in common with genuine socialist concepts. Unless we identify ourselves totally with those fighting for freedom and democracy in the Soviet Union and Eastern Europe our protests against oppression in Chile, Iran, South Africa, etc., are but a sham.

One crucial test for the left is the attitude it takes to those in the Soviet Union who are now trying to create genuine trade unions. At the beginning of 1978 the Free Trade Union Association of the Soviet Working People was founded. As those of their documents included in this collection show, the members of the Association have suffered police harassment, imprisonment and detention in psychiatric hospitals for their attempt to give Soviet workers an independent voice.

The Soviet authorities deny the existence of this Association. Commenting on a report in the *Observer*, Yuri Kornilov of TASS, the official Soviet news agency, declared:

*'All this is twaddle from beginning to end. There are not and never have been any such trade union "associations" in the Soviet Union. As is well known to all, there exist Soviet trade unions which have a membership of over 125,000,000 and enjoy the broadest rights and opportunities for dealing with social and economic tasks.'*

The reality is that trade unions in the Soviet Union are controlled by the state. Consider, for example, the fact that

3

Aleksander Shelepin, who visited Britain as the leader of the Soviet trade unions, was previously head of the KGB, the secret police. Imagine if the former boss of MI5 or MI6 were to become General Secretary of the British TUC!

Socialists have consistently opposed the control of trade unions by the state. They opposed Hitler's absorption of the German unions into the Labour Front, and the transformation of the unions in Mussolini's Italy and Franco's Spain into subordinate parts of the Corporate State. Under Stalin the Soviet trade unions also lost their independence, becoming 'transmission belts' for the bureaucratic party and state machine.

Therefore although trade unions exist in the Soviet Union, with many millions of members, these documents show that they are no longer instruments of workers in their struggle to defend and improve living standards and working conditions. It is perfectly understandable that some independent-minded Soviet workers believe that they must organise genuine trade unions. They should receive the same degree of support from British trade unionists as do trade unionists in Chile, Bolivia, and the black trade unionists of South Africa.

The British labour movement must take a clear stand in support of Soviet trade unionists. If we do not, we will be guilty of the charge of having double standards.

Dr Colin Morris said at a service at Westminster Abbey to commemorate Human Rights Day 1977:

*'We would do well to take account of some words of Gerald Winstanley, leader of the Diggers, a seventeenth century protest movement of the English peasantry against the worldliness of the church and the tyranny of the rich. His followers paid a heavy price for their resistance to the state and from bitter experience he wrote, "There are but few who act for freedom, and the actors are oppressed by the talkers and verbal professors of freedom".'*

Perhaps there has been too much talk about freedom and the time has come to act. An essential part of that action must be to support those in *all* parts of the world who need our help.

*Eric S. Heffer, MP*

4

# The Soviet Working Class

Life is hard in the Soviet Union. It is harder still if you are a worker. You are paid on a piece-rate system: how much is paid per piece is decided by the management in accordance with what it considers to be a reasonable average output per person — the 'norm'. This was introduced during Stalin's first five-year Plan: 29 per cent of workers in 1930 were paid piece-rates; 68 per cent by 1932; by 1949 over 90 per cent.[1]

From the government's point of view this system has two great advantages. First, it destroys collective feeling among the work-force. Every worker is paid according to what *he* or *she* alone produces. Miklos Haraszti, a young Hungarian marxist, describes conditions in a typical East European factory: 'Everyone is on his own. Alone he pursues a daily battle against machines and time. Defeat cannot be shared, how could we want a common success?'

Secondly, as Haraszti says, 'the norms are a rip-off'. They bear no relation to 'the true time taken to make a piece'. 'The rate-fixers cannot but set a production time which demands a super-human effort, since the whole point of norms is to hold wages down to a level fixed in advance'. To earn enough to survive on, the workers have to slave away to fulfil the norm. But once they've done this the norm is readjusted upwards: 'The real meaning of piece-rates lies in the incessant increase in production.'[2] Not only can norms go up — piece-rates can come down. This means that workers have to work harder to earn less. A 30 per cent reduction in piece-rates was one of the things that sparked off the huge strike in Novocherkassk.

A worker's pay-packet is complicated by all sorts of bonuses and supplements to take account of the fact that 'the norm recognises ... no complication in man or materials' (i.e. break-downs in machinery or exceptionally difficult conditions). 'Only one thing is certain: the foremen resist paying supplementary wages'.[3]

5

Then there is the bonus you get when you fulfil the plan, and the extraordinary rhythm the plan dictates to industry. 'Storming to fulfil the monthly, quarterly or annual plan turns every month into a sort of crazy industrial pregnancy, sluggish in gestation and frenzied at the finish'. Yosif, a worker at an air-conditioning and refrigerating plant, explained how at the beginning of the month the workforce is in a state of exhaustion because of the extra work put in to complete the plan, mixed with the effects of drinking off their bonuses. Even when they've recovered, proper work never starts until about the twentieth of the month. They're held up by their suppliers who 'don't fulfil the plan or meet delivery schedules': 'So factories must fulfil about 80 per cent of the plan (quotas) in the last ten or fifteen days.' Extra workers are taken on, shifts are doubled, days-off are cancelled. 'No-one cares any longer about quality. Volume is the main thing.' Any Russian will tell you 'don't buy it if it was made after the twentieth'.[4]

Anatoly Marchenko, a self-educated worker-dissident, has given an unusually dispassionate account of working life in the Siberian settlement of Chuna.[5] At the Chuna timber plant,

*'The average wage of our workers is roughly on a level with the official average wage for the country, i.e. 160 roubles a month. How does the worker earn this sum? In the drying department all the sorting and stacking of planks takes place by hand.... The wet planks that come from the timber mill are five metres long, 19-60mm thick. The norms of output per person (be it a woman or a man) are from 10 to 17 cubic metres a shift, the rate of pay from 23 to 43 kopeks a cubic metre. This means that the worker doesn't earn more than four roubles a shift or 120 roubles a month. Added to this wage is the "supplement for distance" [i.e. the distance from European Russia] — 20 per cent of the wage; and on fulfilment of the plan (an output of over 400 cubic metres a month per person) they pay a bonus. This is how it all adds up to 160 roubles a month. However this wage is not guaranteed. Firstly, the work is so badly organised that the fulfilment of the plan has nothing to do with the individual worker. Secondly, the bonus is only paid if the whole department or shop and not each worker fulfils the monthly plan. The department may fail to fulfil the plan for a thousand reasons which also have nothing to do with the worker. At the end of the month, to fulfil the plan and get the bonus, one has to work an illegal day of seven to eight hours, two*

6

shifts in a row and even on one's days off. These hours are not registered and are not paid as overtime. The illegal additional shifts are organised jointly by the management of the trade unions and the administration. It happens like this because the trade union does not defend the interests of the worker, but those of the state, and fulfilment of the Plan is the chief index of its success ...

'The drying workers work in all weather in the open air, i.e. in winter in more than 40 degrees of frost. According to the law, we should get extra pay for working in freezing conditions — this is known as "the frost supplement". But we aren't paid it here. Our trade union knows this and accepts it.'

Marchenko says that 'most of the work is done by women'. Women make up 51 per cent of the Soviet labour force, while in 1974 they were 53.6 per cent of the population: that is, almost as many women work as men.[6]

Women were drafted into industry under Stalin, not for the sake of sexual equality, but to increase production. Even now, it is they who do most of the unskilled, low-paid jobs. Jobs in the Soviet Union are strictly divided into men's work and women's work. For example, mining and metallurgy are the province of men — only 17 per cent of miners are female. The average wage for miners is 195.3 roubles a month, for metal-workers 129. However, 83 per cent of the workers in light industry are women: 72 per cent of textile workers; 86 per cent of clothing workers; and 74 per cent of bakery and confectionery workers. The average wage in the textile industry is 83.8 roubles a month; in the clothing trades 76.1 roubles; and in the food processing industries 92.7 roubles. Almost all teachers (72 per cent) and health workers (84 per cent) are female.[7] These too are badly paid and poorly regarded jobs in the Soviet Union.

In many industries men do the skilled jobs, women the heavy, dirty, unskilled ones. On collective farms it is the men who drive the tractors, the women who dig the fields; in summer it is the women who sweep the streets with long birch brooms; in winter it is the women who scrape the snow and ice off the pavements with long tin shovels. In the machine industry 67 per cent of women work in the least skilled grades — I and II — and only 23 per cent of men. Only 5.5 per cent of women reach grades IV to VI, over 50 per cent of men.[8] In the evenings, many men go to night school to get higher qualifications: the women stay at home to do the housework and

7

look after the children. Soviet sociological studies show that women often do over 80 per cent of the housework with no help from anyone.[9]

The Soviet government may boast with some justification about its almost free nurseries and kindergartens, but there are only enough of them for a third of the children of pre-school age.[10] Mothers are allowed 112 paid days off for pregnancy, and an optional unpaid year after birth with their job guaranteed. However most of them, nursery or no nursery, go straight back to work. As Soviet experts admit, the reason is money. Marchenko explains how they manage at Chuna:

*'There are only day nurseries and kindergartens in Chuna. To avoid leaving their children alone, married couples arrange to work on different shifts; they see each other in passing. It's even worse for single mothers: they have to leave their small children without any supervision in the evenings. A female friend of mine tells me that her children (seven and ten years old) can't get to sleep until she comes back from the second shift, i.e. until two o'clock in the morning.'*

The alternative is to manage on one salary. Can this be done? In 1975 the legal minimum wage was 70 roubles, the average wage (for manual and non-manual workers) 146 roubles a month. This is before income tax and other deductions (about 14 roubles).[11] How little this is can be seen from the fact that the official Soviet poverty level is *50 roubles a head*. A survey of the incomes of 10,000 working-class families in Leningrad (1961-65) revealed that 40 per cent of them fell below this level.[12] The situation is naturally worst for large families: child allowances introduced during the war cover only a small part of the expenses of raising children, as Sery, a father of seven, complains (pp.109-10). As for pensioners, in 1974 they got an average of 40 roubles a month.[13]

Food in the state shops is neither good nor cheap. And it's scarce. Butter, milk and eggs are often unobtainable. It's only in very privileged cities like Moscow and Leiningrad that meat can be found all the year round. The disastrous harvest of 1975 made things much worse. Now every Thursday (and sometimes every Tuesday as well) the canteens, cafes and restaurants only serve fish. The 'average Soviet citizen still gets about half of his daily calories from bread and potatoes and eats less than half as much meat as do his counterparts in the US and Western Europe'.[14] For most of

8

the winter the only vegetable available is frost-bitten cabbage. When a delivery of something else appears (oranges, for example) queues appear like magic in the street — you join the queue first, ask afterwards what you're queuing for.

The other source of food is the private market. This sells produce grown on the tiny patches of land (up to one acre) which private citizens are still legally allowed to own. There are estimated to be about 50 million of these — providing 64 per cent of the country's potatoes; 45 per cent of the eggs; 40 per cent of the vegetables; 31 per cent of the meat; and 33 per cent of the milk (1971 figures).[15] The markets sell food of much higher quality and greater variety — but it costs two or three times as much as in the state shops.

What about other goods? The five-year plan on 1971-5, which aimed to remedy the imbalance between consumer and industrial goods, was a disastrous flop. Marchenko says that his 160 roubles will buy 'one and a half suits; or a third of a black-and-white TV; or one aeroplane ticket from Chuna to Moscow and back; or two wheels for a baby car "Moskvich"; or three to five children's coats'. (Soviet clothes are very expensive and very nasty.)

Inflation is largely suppressed — it is just reflected in shortages. But in 1977 the cost of air travel went up by 30 per cent; the price of books doubled; the price of a car rose by 1,000 roubles to 8,000 roubles (about £6,000 — and you may have to wait years for one).

What about technical gadgets to help the working woman in the home? A survey of a group of women factory workers in Leningrad and the nearby industrial town of Kostroma showed just how few possessed ordinary household aids.[16]

|  | Leningrad | Kostroma |
|---|---|---|
|  | per cent | per cent |
| refrigerators | 0.4 | 13.5 |
| washing machines | — | 16.8 |
| sewing machines | 5.1 | 35.0 |
| floor polishers | 2.0 | 0.4 |
| vacuum cleaners | 11.5 | 1.6 |

Only 10 per cent of these women ever used the public

laundries, which they said took weeks and sent their clothes back torn or not at all (there aren't any laundrettes).[17] Good-quality consumer goods can be found only in the ubiquitous black market, at extortionate prices (100 roubles — about £80 — for a pair of Western jeans), or in the foreign-currency shops reserved for tourists and party officials.

Almost all Soviet citizens live in flats. The Soviet leaders say they are building apartments for their workers as fast as they can. They claim that 'the Soviet Union completes work on five modern flats every minute. This rate has been maintained for several years in succession' (1975).[18] However this isn't fast enough: 'in 1965 the shortfall of units built was 142,097 but by 1974 it had reached a staggering 1.1. million units'.[19] All around the big cities stand the *novye raioni* (new districts) — grey, grim concrete tower blocks surrounded by waste-land, with no grass, and no shops as yet. These, at least, have sanitation, running water and central heating; rent, gas and electricity bills are minimal. Other workers, however, live in appalling conditions.

Andrey Sakharov, a leading dissident who has recently turned his attention to the plight of the workers, claims that 'The water situation is bad. Most cities and towns do not have a modern sewage system'.[20] This view was backed up by the 24th Congress of the CPSU which laid down that 'a central water supply and water piping is to be laid on in 700 towns and workers' settlements during the five-year period' (1971-5).[21] This plan was not fulfilled.

Marchenko describes housing conditions in a typical Soviet small town:

*'It is said, that we have the cheapest housing in the world. Rent takes one eighth to a tenth of the average wage. My friend pays 17 roubles a month for his flat. He and his wife, their two working daughters and schoolboy son live in the flat. It has two adjoining rooms (16 and 12 cubic metres) with a tiny — (you can hardly squeeze your way through) — corridor, an equally tiny kitchen and bathroom. Their house — a big building divided up into flats — has conveniences: central heating, an electric stove in the kitchen, hot and cold water and sewerage. This is the maximum comfort known to us.*

*'Roughly a quarter of the population of Chuna lives in such houses. Half of the two-storied houses, each of which is divided*

*into six flats, don't have any conveniences: they have only one lavatory—a cold wooden hut in the yard; water comes from a pump in the street; the stove is the only source of heating.*

*'The rest of the inhabitants of the village live in little houses, either their own or the state's. These of course don't have any convenience either. Often the water doesn't even come from a pump, but from a well which you have to work by hand, several hundred metres from the house.'*

People need somewhere to live, just as they need something to eat. And so, once more, the private sector steps in. 'As late as 1975 some 30 per cent of all new housing space (measured in square metres) was completed by non-state entities: housing co-operatives, collective farms, and individuals, with the last having far the greatest share.' [22] Such houses are built largely with materials and labour stolen from the state, and the prices and rents charged for them are enormous.

What matters almost as much as having a home is where it is. Most people want to live in the big cities. These have the meat, the fresh vegetables, and the consumer goods, that the rest of the country lacks. They are privileged areas, entry to which is strictly controlled by the authorities. Every citizen has an internal passport which contains a residence permit, giving permission to live in a limited area. He or she can move only with the agreement of the powers that be. Entry to cities like Moscow and Leningrad is granted only to those who are prepared to work their way in by slaving for a couple of years at digging the roads or repainting the Winter Palace in 20 degrees of frost. As a result, all cities have thousands of illegal residents. (These controls particularly affect citizens who, against the wishes of the authorities, come to petition the central government.)

Life is not so good for those who fall ill either:

*'Medical care for the majority of the population is of a low quality. It takes half a day to see a doctor at a clinic and what can the doctor do or understand in the ten minutes he has for seeing each patient? ... At the hospitals the patients lie in corridors where either the air is stuffy or else there is a draught. There are no "sick-nurses", few orderlies or practical nurses, and a handful of registered nurses. The situation is bad with regard to their medication and food. For an ordinary hospital, the budget allocates less than one rouble per day per patient for everything. Naturally,*

11

*there is nothing and conditions are frightful ... Those unquestionable gains made by medicine in the first decade of the Soviet regime (in paediatrics, in combating infectious diseases etc.) are now threatened.'*[23]

Marchenko reminds us that it's not so bad for the elite:

*'If one of the especially equal falls ill he gets special medical treatment as well. There will even be room for him in a separate ward and he won't have to suffer from shortages of medicine and food at 50 kopeks a day like the ordinary patients.'*

In Moscow there are even special hospitals for bureaucrats.

The education workers receive is much better than it has ever been. In 1926 less than half the women in the country could read, and the rate was only slightly higher for men. By 1959 it had risen to almost 100 per cent for both sexes.[24] But it is still an old-fashioned, disciplined, highly selective system. The boys wear little grey army suits, the girls black dresses and white frilly aprons left over from Tsarist times. They have lots of homework. In spite of this, there's general agreement with Marchenko about 'how low the general standard of education is in our schools'.

Most working-class children don't stay on for the last two years of school (the figures for Gorky region show that only 1.5 per cent of pupils in the 10th and 11th classes — the highest grades — are children of unskilled manual workers[25]). The best education is to be had in special schools, which it takes a great deal of string-pulling to get into. It seems to be difficult for workers to get into university. There are no figures, but according to a recent estimate only 10 to 20 per cent of students at Moscow and Leningrad Universities are of worker or peasant stock (Khruschev put it only as high as 30 to 40 per cent for all the higher education institutions is Moscow).[26]

Workers in the West also live under a class-biased social system. They have organised trade unions to fight for improvements in their material situation. This alternative is not open to Soviet workers, however — the trade unions are an instrument of the state.

Trade union membership is theoretically voluntary, but in 1972 97.5 per cent of the employed were trade union members. Soviet trade unions are industrial unions and cover the whole of the USSR (in 1972 there were 25 of them). The Second Congress of Trade Unions (1919) adopted the 'production principle', which means that manual and non-manual workers in one enterprise are in the same union. Their actual job is irrelevant — an electrician will be attached to the coal-mining union if he works in a coal-mine, or to the railway union if he works on the railways.

In the early years of the twentieth century trade unions were composed almost entirely of manual workers. However, at the time of the revolution professional people and clerical workers were drawn in; and later (in the 1930s) also the higher technical and administrative personnel, including industrial managers whose standing in relation to the workers was that of employers.

The unions are organised in much the same way as the Communist Party — in factory committees, town committees, regional committees, and so on up to the All-Union Central Council of Trade Unions. This body operates, in the words of the marxist historian Isaac Deutscher, on the principle of 'bureaucratic rather than democratic centralism. The power of the centre is practically unlimited, and the standing provisions about the responsibility of the trade union officials to their electorate are disregarded'.[27] For example, there was a 17-year gap between the 10th Congress of Trade Unions in 1932 and the 11th in 1949. The Central Council didn't even bother to go through the formal motions of an election in the meantime. The head of the trade unions is in fact appointed by the government. The last one, Aleksander Shelepin, was previously Chairman of the KGB (the secret police). His successor is Shibaev, previously First Secretary of the Saratov Regional Party Committee.

In the enterprise the factory committee is chosen by the management, not by the workers. The members of the Free Trade Union Association give a detailed description of how elections are rigged (see pp.31-34). There are collective agreements between management and trade unions. But if you read them you will find that the main task of the union seems to be not to defend the workers' interests, but to discipline them and make sure they fulfil the plan. For example, the agreement for the Zaprozhtal Iron and Steel Works (1975) begins: 'In order to ensure the fulfilment of the plan ahead of time ...'; and goes on, 'The management and the trade union committee undertake: to examine every infringement of labour discipline (absenteeism, lateness, breakdown of equipment, production of faulty goods etc.) and breach of public order at meetings of trade union groups and shop trade union committees...

Disciplinary measures shall be applied by the management in concert with the trade union organisation'. These measures include: 'the refusal of material assistance from the incentive fund to such workers; the refusal of accommodation at holiday homes, sanatoria and the plant's clinic; the deferral of the granting of housing to a later date and of the annual leave to winter'.[28]

The trade union's secondary task, which it carries out through various commissions, is to organise social insurance, cultural and educational activities, housing, holidays, etc. Deutscher sums up:

*'As the organisation designed to forge the workers' solidarity in their struggle for better living conditions, they have suffered complete atrophy. As bodies entrusted with the management of social insurance and as welfare institutions, they have certainly performed and are still performing very useful services; but these, whatever the official Soviet theory may be, they have performed as subsidiaries of the State administration, not as autonomous social bodies or working-class organs in the accepted sense.'[29]*

A further severe restraint on workers' rights is the 'labour book' which every worker has to carry. This contains details of his or her work record, and without it no worker can obtain a job.

Strike action, the traditional weapon used by workers to defend their material interests, is not, in theory, illegal in the Soviet Union. In practice, however, the unions, the management and the state collude to prevent strikes from taking place. When they occur, as at Novocherkassk in 1962, strikes tend to take the form of sudden, spontaneous outbursts of anger — resentments that have accumulated over years suddenly explode. Very often strikes are fiercely repressed — at Novocherkassk the strikers were mowed down with dum-dum bullets. (See section two *The Right to Strike*, pp.76-81.)

Other forms of resistance take place within the factories. 'Italian-style strikes' — silent sit-ins — are common. Go-slows are, however, more popular:

*'One man, who later became an engineer, said that when he was 17, being taught by an older worker how to operate a lathe, he asked whether it could not be operated faster. "Yes, but shut up", the older man said. "Next month they are revising the norms, so we slowed it down on purpose".'[30]*

And almost every worker pilfers, drinks and tries to avoid work. 'The right not to work hard at the factory is one of the few

14

remaining rights that the Soviet worker holds.'[31]

It is in this context that the documents in this book must be seen. They are the voice of a working class denied all means of organised self-expression. The rights guaranteed in the Soviet Constitution — 'freedom of speech, of the press, and of assembly' (article 50), 'the right to associate in public organisations' (article 51), 'freedom of conscience' (article 52) — are a dead letter.

In Britain and other Western countries traditions of collective organisation and solidarity built up over decades of struggle form the basis of a strong labour movement. In the USSR there are no such traditions still alive. No independent workers' organisations have been seen there since the 1920s. The emergence of the tiny, persecuted Free Trade Union Association led by Vladimir Klebanov, can therefore be seen as a turning point in Soviet history.

The political ideas of these working-class dissidents are still in the melting-pot. Their lack of working-class traditions and the absence of open political life in the USSR, makes them liable to admire life in the West, where the workers have political and trade union rights, and in comparison with them seem rich. This is only natural. It is not a reason for workers in the West to withhold support from the Free Trade Union Association. The road to socialist democracy and an authentic workers' state in the Soviet Union lies through the fight for basic political and trade union rights, the fight for a better standard of living. This fight can only succeed if organisations like the FTUA spread to the mass of Soviet workers. For this, the support of Western trade unionists is vital.

# 1:

# The Right to Organise
## Introduction:
## The Free Trade Union Association
## of the Soviet Working People

The idea of forming an independent trade union seems to have come from Vladimir Klebanov, a skilled mining engineer from the Ukraine. Also a local trade union organiser, his troubles began when he tried to defend the interests of his fellow miners. His incredible persistence and determination enabled him to survive a pitched battle against the authorities which he began in 1958, and which is still going on.

The West first heard of the Free Trade Union Association (FTUA) on 25 November 1977, when Klebanov held a first informal press conference in Moscow in a flat belonging to Nikolayev, the one intellectual member of the group. Klebanov and ten others held a second press conference on 10 January 1978; and on 26 January, Klebanov and six others announced that 200 workers were ready to join. On 1 February they gave foreign correspondents the statutes of the Free Trade Union Association of the Soviet Working People, a list of 110 candidate members, and their *Appeal to the International Labour Organisation and Trade Unions in the West*. They asked for international solidarity, trade union recognition and financial aid.

So far, nine sets of documents have reached the West. The first is dated 20 May 1977, the last February 1978. They are appeals on behalf of Soviet workers who have fallen foul of management and party officials.

These people are not 'dissidents' in the normal sense of the word. They are much simpler men and women, 'honest labourers of the socialist society, producers of national wealth'. They come from all strata of the working class; they include Klebanov, the skilled foreman, and Poplavsky, chief of a factory department, as

16

well as Ivanov, the bulldozer driver, and Shkorbatov, the night watchman. They come from all parts of the country from Riga to Vladivostok. A high proportion are from the Ukraine, a traditional centre of working class political opposition to the regime, and Klebanov's home area. Almost half of them are women — 20 out of the 43 publicly-known members, 49 out of 110 candidate members.

They are ordinary people, who were taught in school, in the Komsomol, and in the army, that the Soviet system was the best in the world. For the most part they believed what they were told. Their problems began at work. They saw managers furthering their careers by bribery, swindling, stealing 'socialist property', concealing industrial accidents, paying illegally low wages, and so on. As 'honest labourers' they stood up to defend socialist property, to demand proper implementation of the Labour Code and the Constitution. Their reward for their loyalty was the sack.

They discovered the truth behind the official propaganda about 'the right to work' — it is granted by the ruling bureaucrats to those who behave. Officially, there is no unemployment in the Soviet Union, so there is no unemployment pay. The members of the Free Trade Union Association say, 'We are the great army of Soviet unemployed, thrown outside the factory gates for exercising our right to complain, our right to criticise and our right to free speech.' They claim that this army numbers 'tens of thousands, even hundreds of thousands'. The rest are, understandably, afraid to come out into the open.

They petitioned to get their jobs back. The wall of bureaucratic solidarity confronted them once more. Their petitions were sent to 'the very organs against which we are complaining'. The exceptionally persistent who carried their grievances to Moscow were rewarded with searches, beatings, prison and psychiatric hospital.

Their reaction to this was the same as that of the Russian peasant before the Russian revolution: our system is good, our rulers are good, but wicked officials are perverting things for their own personal ends. Just as the peasants addressed their complaints against the landowners to the Tsar (the 'Little Father'), so the Soviet workers, directly and by rousing world opinion, appeal to Brezhnev. They demand audience with 'the leaders of the *Party* and *Government* who are barred from us by the barrier of Bureaucracy'.[1] They are not admirers of capitalism, and often apologise

17

for the fact that they 'have been compelled to appeal to ... the bourgeois press'.

Their respect for the Soviet system, their innocence and lack of any real political analysis lead these workers to link their problems very closely with traditional Soviet dissidence, the civil rights movement directed by members of the intelligentsia. They do not call for revolution but for observance of the law. The aim of their trade union is to fight for the rights the official trade unions don't defend at the workplace. When they fail to get justice in the Soviet Union, they appeal to what they consider to be higher authorities — the United Nations, the Belgrade Conference reviewing the Helsinki Agreement, Jimmy Carter, and the International Labour Organisation. They want them to tell Brezhnev what is going on, make him punish the wicked bureaucrats and implement the Constitution.

What distinguishes these workers from the civil rights movement and what makes them so important, is, first of all, that their complaints stem *from the workplace*: their original criticisms are *economic*.

Secondly, they are organised. The Free Trade Union Association is the first independent workers' organisation formed in the Soviet Union since the 1920s. The official All-Union Central Council of Trade Unions (AUCCTU) is run by the Communist Party, i.e. by the government. All AUCCTU officials are Communist Party members, chosen by and completely dependent on the management, who hold higher Communist Party positions. The *Appeal to the ILO* gives us a vivid description of exactly how trade union 'elections' take place, and how workers are systematically excluded from union positions.

It's no good trying to complain through your trade union in the Soviet Union. There is no right to strike, no right to demonstrate. The only complaining possible is individual complaining: you write a declaration (called a Zayavleniye) stating your own individual grievance, you stand in a queue, and eventually present it to some faceless bureaucrat, whose 'sole concern is how to get rid of the complainant'. Every despotism knows that the individual is easy to deal with.

When the local bureaucrats throw you out, if you're brave you can go to Moscow.[2] They won't give you a permit to live there so you'll have to 'hang about in railway stations'.[3] The men and

18

women who were to form the Free Trade Union Association met in the Waiting Room of the Central Committee of the CPSU. Those who stand in these queues too long are hustled out by the police to be imprisoned, committed to mental hospitals, or simply kicked out of Moscow. On one occasion 'before the eyes of hundreds of citizens from various cities across the country, one petitioner, driven to despair, committed suicide' (16 April 1975).

Finally, exasperated, the petitioners got together and 'decided to organise our own genuinely independent trade unions'. The Free Trade Union Association is the union of the oppressed against the exploiters at the workplace. Any worker, skilled or unskilled, from any branch of industry, can join, so long as 'his rights and interests have been illegally flouted'. In this it's a reflection of the official trade unions, which are industrial unions — their membership includes all trades of workers, and most of the management too. However, very differently, the Free Trade Union Association's statutes lay down that 'all officials from top to bottom are elected by members' at a general meeting. The union has 43 public members, and another 200 who don't want their names to be known, for obvious reasons. There are also 110 candidate members — other workers whose cases the FTUA has taken up.

The Free Trade Union Association seems to have been under attack from the moment it was born. Its founders discovered that 'on 20 January 1978, lists of the names of the citizens who had signed the *Open Letter to International Opinion* (18 September 1977) were distributed to all the police stations in Moscow'.[4] Since 1 February there have been many reports of arrest, imprisonment and detention in psychiatric hospitals. Vladimir Poplavsky, for example, was sentenced on 18 May to one year's imprisonment for 'parasitism', that is, for refusing to work. In reality, he had been sacked in 1975 for 'exposing the abuses of the factory management' and has since been fighting for the right to work. A.M.Boiko, F.P.Dvoretsky, V.Garvrilenko, M.S.Gudz, V.I. Korchagin, P.M.Mur'yov, V.Y.Nikitin, Y.B.Nikolayev, and V.V. Shcherbakov, are all at present (July 1978) in psychiatric hospitals. Klebanov has been transferred from a psychiatric hospital to a prison.

In April 1978 the Free Trade Union Association's lawyer Vsevolod Kuvakin thanked the French trade unions for their support and announced that 'despite the repression of some of the

Association's members, the unofficial trade union movement is still active and continues its work'. It seems, however, that the group decided to protect itself by moving underground: 'unlike previous statements, the most recent statement was not signed by all the members of the Association "in order not to needlessly compromise our comrades"'.[5]

The ultimate fate of the members of the Free Trade Union Association depends on several things. The first is the balance of power inside the Soviet Union. There are small, but important signs of a gradual shift against the rulers. The leaders of the civil rights movement are being persecuted, but support for them is growing amongst the intelligentisa. There are also indications that the Russian in the street is losing some of his or her fear of the authorities. Not only do some workers dare to speak out against the management, but passers-by are prepared to step forward in their defence and even fight the police to save them from arrest. When the Klim police forced their way into Taisiya Kategorenko's flat, her 'son Gennady, and the neighbours showed them the door'. (See p.51). The growth of working class solidarity is especially obvious in the case of Klebanov, who was several times saved by the action of the miners of Makeyevka. The authorities had to transfer 'hundreds of workers to other pits' before they dared arrest him.

Secondly, international solidarity action has always had a crucial influence on the fate of oppositionists in the Soviet Union. Soviet workers naturally turn to workers' organisations abroad. But if these are unresponsive or support the Soviet government, they are forced to appeal to the capitalists and their political organisations.

The Free Trade Union Association has asked the ILO and the Western trade unions for recognition and moral and financial support. What has been the response? The ILO waited until November 1978 before launching a full-scale investigation.[6]

In Britain the TUC General Council has decided not to support the Free Trade Union Association after receiving a reply from the Soviet All-Union Trade Union Council. In a letter to Len Murray, General Secretary of the TUC, A.I. Shibayev, head of the Soviet trade unions, stated that 'the Soviet trade unions do not see any reason to support a group of this kind', which he describes as not a trade union but an 'organisation of complainers'. In a subsequent letter to Ron Hayward, General Secretary of the

Labour Party, Murray indicated the TUC's satisfaction with Shibayev's reply, stating that the General Council felt it had been 'directed to the substance of the matter'.

In the International Confederation of Free Trade Unions (ICFTU) the two votes against making a formal complaint to the ILO were those of the Canadian representative, and Jack Jones, former General Secretary of the British Transport and General Workers Union. (They argued that there was not enough evidence!)

The emergence of the Free Trade Union Association led to a debate on the Soviet Union at the annual Trade Union Congress at Brighton in September 1978. Two resolutions were passed — one a declaration of general support for a charter of human rights, the other backing the establishment of free trade unions anywhere and denouncing the use of psychiatric treatment to repress trade union independence.

However, the TUC did not offer support to the FTUA. Bill Sirs, of the Iron and Steel Trades Confederation, moving the resolution on free trade unionism, accepted the regime's argument that the FTUA was not a proper trade union since it did not organise workers in a specific industry. The trade union movement in Britain 'would not stand for such a move where other unions existed. Why should British trade unionists expect the Russians to?' Thus the TUC continues to accept the legitimacy of the official Soviet trade unions.

A more positive stance has been taken by the French labour movement. The leaders of the Confédération Générale du Travail (CGT — Communist trade union federation), the Confédération Française Démocratique du Travail (CFDT — pro-Socialist union federation), and the Fédération de l'Éducation Nationale (FEN — teachers' union), have come out in full solidarity with the Association. At a press conference held on 18 April 1978 the CFDT representative demanded the immediate release of Klebanov and reaffirmed his organisation's support of the struggle for democratic rights in the East. The CGT spokesperson condemned the 'violation of the democratic rights and liberties of individual trade unionists and trade union collectives in the Soviet Union'.[7]

Some sections of the British labour movement have also expressed solidarity with the FTUA, notably the Amalgamated Union of Engineering Workers (AUEW), Engineering Section; the Transport and General Workers Union (TGWU); the National

21

Union of Mineworkers (NUM); the National Union of Railwaymen (NUR); the National Association of Local Government Officers (NALGO); the National Graphical Association (NGA); the Union of Shop, Distributive, and Allied Workers (USDAW); the Boilermarkers (ASBSBSW); and the National Woolsorters Society. Moreover, on 25 July 1978 the National Executive Committee of the Labour Party passed a resolution stating that it 'supports those workers in the Soviet Union who wish to organise free and independent trade unions on a basis similar to those that exist in Britain, France, Italy, and so on' and welcoming the ILO investigation of the ICFTU complaint.

The Soviet Government's first response to international protests was to deny the existence of the Free Trade Union Association (TASS, official Soviet news agency, 21 April 1978). Then, when the ICFTU and the World Confederation of Labour raised the issue at the ILO, the World Confederation of Trade Unions (international body of Eastern bloc and pro-Communist trade unions) issued a statement entitled *Against slanderous attacks on socialist countries*. It said,

*'The organisers of the slanderous attacks are interfering in the internal affairs of other trade union centres. They are trying to mislead the international trade union movement by showing that a so-called "alternative trade union movement" exists in the socialist block. In reality these people are renegades — "dissidents" who have absolutely no connection with the workers or trade unions in these countries.'*[10]

The documents prove the opposite...

# Selected Documents of
the Free Trade Union Association
of the Soviet Working People[11]

★ Document 1 / 20 May 1977
Open Letter
To International Opinion

We are Soviet citizens from various towns of the Soviet Union — united in bitterness.

We have been unjustly deprived of work — sacked and left without means of livelihood. The only response we get to our questions is continuous persecution. As far as propaganda about human rights is concerned everything is well arranged here.

In the press, issue after issue for months in a row can publish stories about the kindness and humanity shown to someone's lost dog. On the other hand not a single paper will accept our declarations which have to do with the human sufferings of honest citizens and their children — people who for many years have been living a life much worse than a *dog* in an *airport*.

Wherever we turn — to the Procurator's Office of the USSR, the Supreme Court of the USSR, the Council of Ministers of the USSR, the Presidium of the Supreme Soviet of the USSR, the All-Union Central Council of Trade Unions and the Central Committee of the Communist Party of the Soviet Union — *everywhere* we are refused even a hearing, and our complaints are sent to the very organs against which we are lodging complaints. Or we are fobbed off with formal rejections.

The only reason for this is that we are decent, principled people who have come out against bribery, swindling, theft of socialist property, concealment of industrial accidents and other abuses by managers at the enterprises where we *used to work*.

We envy that anonymous *dog* living at the airport; it received tender human care — not insults and destitution ...

We on the other hand, who bear surname, forenames and have children who bear our patronymics — *we are suffering*. We are undeservedly insulted, beaten up, thrown into jail and psychiatric hospitals.

A dog would not have borne the kind of humiliation and derision we have suffered.

[Here follow eight case histories]

People are not animals!

Certain immoral men protect those who steal state property, and have formed themselves into a ring for their mutual advantage. Whether they like it or not — we announce to all honest Soviet citizens the names of those innocent people who have at various times been shut up in prisons and psychiatric *hospitals*.

[35 names and addresses are listed]

There is a saying: 'A fish rots from the head!'

[*Signed by eight people*]

★ Document 2 / 18 September 1977
Open Letter
To International Opinion
on the True Situation of Workers and Employees
on the Eve of the 60th Anniversary of the USSR

The following open letter is for publicity purposes.

Copy: *To the United Nations*

Copy: *To the Belgrade Conference of Heads of Governments for bringing to the attention of the leaders of the Soviet delegation*

In the past ten years important changes of an ideological and political nature have taken place within the USSR with the aim of increasing her prestige abroad and of erasing from the popular memory the bloody consequences of the cult of Stalin and Khrushchev. These changes, however, are not simply of significance for propaganda and raising the prestige of the Communist Party of the Soviet Union in the eyes of world opinion. They also have important implications for the working people inside the country. The measures include renewing party cards as Vladimir Ilich did, and the increased prestige given to the word 'citizen' by the new passport system.[12]

On 9 September 1977, member of the Politburo of the CC CPSU and Chairman of the KGB of the USSR, Yu.V.Andropov, stated:

'*Our starting point is this, that the individual enjoys complete freedom as long as his activities are in harmony with the general direction of social progress ...*

*'Soviet laws allow every citizen very wide political freedoms ...*

*'Those comrades, who come forward with constructive critic-isms desiring to further the general cause we treat as conscientious critics and we thank them.*

*'Those whose criticisms are mistaken, we treat as misguided people ...*

*'And finally ... Some Western politicians throw at us the (in their opinion) clever question: "Why on the sixtieth anniversary of the Soviet Union do so-called 'dissidents' still exist in the USSR?".
... As has already been said, we try to help the erring — we try to change their minds, and correct their errors.*

*'However, we have reached a situation where the activities of some of these so-called "dissidents" run counter to Soviet laws ... Some people reject our society and choose the path of anti-Soviet activity — they break the law, supply the West with slanderous information, spread false rumours, and attempt to organise various anti-social attacks ... These renegades are not and cannot be tolerated in our country.'*

We are Soviet people from different sections of society, who did not know each other before, but who have met on the crossroads of suffering in the full sense of the word. We are people from various nationalities and from different parts of the country who have been compelled to appeal to the so-called 'bourgeois press'. We honest labourers of the socialist society, producers of material wealth, are ignored by our leaders, our press, the party and soviet organs, whose function and obligation it is to hear us and to resolve our problems.

### How Many are We?

We think we are tens of thousands, hundreds of thousands. We will not produce high-flowing words. We will simply describe our ordinary, human misfortunes and sufferings.

Today we are suffering — tomorrow any citizen of the USSR may become a member of our collective and think as we do.

Everything is very simple: the ruling elite is doing everything it can to break us up and crush us morally and physically.

With whatever problem a Soviet person appeals — to the Procurator's Office, the People's Courts, the ministries, the Presidium of the Supreme Soviet, the press, the All-Union Central Council of Trade Unions, and in the last resort to the Central Committee of the CPSU — everywhere the guardians of the law proceed not from the dictates of the law, but from their own personal interests.

We are middle-aged people and each of us has shouldered more than a dozen years of work experience in various productive collectives. We were front rank workers. And so it is quite natural that we have a real right to think and speak on our own behalf, and on behalf of our comrades at work. All they have to do is to speak out in public against wasters of socialist property, poor working conditions, low pay, high rates of injury at work, speed-up and increased output norms, leading to wastage and low quality production, the continuous rise in the price of basic necessities and foodstuffs, and all that with us is called 'shortages' and 'temporary difficulties' — and they will at once join our ranks.

We consider ourselves obliged for our own sake and for theirs, to inform the world of the real situation with regard to our right to freedom and the defence of our rights — how the constitution is observed in reality, and what happens when we complain to persons in authority.

We are the great army of Soviet unemployed, thrown outside the factory gates for exercising our right of complaint, our right to criticise and our right to free speech.

Our press, radio and television widely publicises despotism and violence in the rest of the world, but in our free country no-one will stand up in our defence and make known the hunger and destitution suffered by us and our children.

Any reasonable person will understand that it is impossible to talk about hundreds or thousands of human beings. But by describing a few dozen cases of ordinary human suffering, we can demonstrate convincingly that any Soviet citizen may share the fate of tens of thousands of people who have appealed to the same organs and organisations, and in particular, to the same officials — men who, by virtue of their interests, principles and practices, are capable of responding in only one way.

A massive amount of evidence of despotism and coercion has piled up, and it is not of an accidental nature. For wherever a worker or employee works, wherever he lives, whatever institution he complains to, in the last analysis all roads lead to the same functionaries and to the repressive measures which they bring to bear on citizens seeking justice or protection from the law.

We will describe our authentic cases, based on documents and real events. [Here follow 22 case histories]

We consider the statement of the Chairman of the KGB, Yu.V.Andropov — that in our country they try to help people — false. Perhaps putting complainants in psychiatric hospitals and special detention centres in Moscow is what they call 'changing their minds' and 'correcting' their errors. If so, it's a barbaric and inhuman method.

The names of the honest Soviet citizens whom they have tried to 'correct and re-educate' must be made known to all Soviet people and to world opinion. [Here follow 50 brief case histories]

In protest against the arbitrary treatment to which they have been subjected, the following citizens, quite independently of each other asked the Presidium of the Supreme Soviet of the USSR for the termination of their Soviet citizenship. [23 names listed]

None of the above-mentioned are renegades, and none of them has committed any anti-social act. Neither have they supplied the West with slanderous information or spread false rumours. Yet some of them were put in psychiatric hospitals and turned out of Moscow, simply because they came to Moscow with complaints about unjust dismissals or demands for better living conditions, etc.

Wherever a Soviet citizen appeals in search of justice, no-one wants to hear. Their sole concern is how to get rid of the complainant.

To this purpose the police and KGB spare no effort in support of the bureaucratic apparatus. They drag you to the police station singly and in groups.

On 12 July 1977 they treated one group of citizens like this: Mikhail Yegorovich Gur'ev, Mikhail Leonidovich Melent'ev, Nikolay Pavlovich Ivanov, and Varvara Ivanovna Kucherenko were seized in the Waiting Room of the Central Committee of the CPSU and taken to Moscow Police Station No.46, where they were ordered to give a written undertaking never to show up at the Central Committee again.

In Moscow there are a series of special detention centres, administered by a Board of Internal Affairs, for ridding Moscow of petitioners. There they try at first to frighten petitioners by imprisoning them and subjecting them to humiliating searches. For example Special Detention Centre No.2 of the Board of Internal Affairs of the Moscow City Executive Committee is situated on

Novoslabodsky Street, House 45, Building 4. Its chief is senior police lieutenant P.Yefimov. There they have blank warrants of arrest. A particularly large number of these are distributed to the Waiting Room of the All-Union Central Council of Trade Unions.

Employees of the administrative organs of the Central Committee of the CPSU, the Supreme Soviet, Procurator's Office, etc., deceive petitioners by saying that they've run out of money and go off home. Some of these employees are: CPSU — Deputy Head of Department Victor Ivanovich Gladyshchev, Head of Sector Sergei Aleksandrovich Shishkov, senior officials Lev Dmitriyevich Smirnov, Nikolay Aleksandrovich Petukhov, A.V.Titov, Potapenko, Shchukin, and others; Head of the Waiting Room of the Central Committee V.N.Filatov; Head of the Waiting Room of the Presidium of the Supreme Soviet Mikhail Petrovich Sklyarov; Head of the Waiting Room of the Procurator's Office of the USSR Nikolai Vasil'evich Tsybul'nikov; Procurator Irina Ilinichna Klochkova; First Deputy of the General Procurator of the USSR Aleksandr Mikhailovich Rekunkov; Deputy General Procurator of the USSR Aleksandr Semyonovich Pankratov; Heads of Department V.I.Zamyatin, I.V.Chermensky, Kudryavtsev, and others.

They have made use of the lack of control exercised by the leaders of the Party and Government to create a tightly-organised ring for their mutual advantage — they give empty, formal replies, harass people, put them in psychiatric hospitals, etc.

The editors of the national newspapers, *Pravda, Trud, Izvestia, Literaturnaya Gazeta*, etc. are completely dependent on and controlled by the Central Committee of the CPSU.

We are not afraid of being tried in our workplaces; we are not afraid of open courts. If we are wrong, let us be judged — but openly with the participation of the workers. And we are convinced that the workers will judge not us but the Gladyshchevs, Shishkovs, Filatovs, Pankratovs, Rekunkovs — and put them in the dock instead!

We do not consider that giving wide publicity to the evidence of tyrannical and arbitrary practices, and bringing it to the attention of international opinion constitutes an interference in the internal affairs of the Soviet Union.

We earnestly beg you to present our statement to international opinion so that the world may know at the Belgrade Conference of Heads of States, the signatories of the Helsinki Agreement may know, above all, exactly where *human rights* are being trampled on.

*We ask your assistance in the resolution of our complaints in accordance with the law and constitution of the Soviet Union and to put an end to the persecution and harassment of citizens.*

Note: Copies of this open letter will be sent to the Soviet Government and the Central Committee of the CPSU and the national press of the Soviet Union.

[*Signed by 25 people*]

★ **Document 3 / 1 February 1978**
Appeal
To the International Labour Organisation (ILO)
and to Trade Unions in the West

We are unemployed Soviet workers, who have come to Moscow from various cities and republics of the country. We are forced to seek moral and material support through this Appeal in the Western press. No other possibilities remain open to us.

We have all been dismissed for exposing abuses or for speaking out against the management of the enterprises where we worked. Among the issues we raised were pilfering and dilutions of materials, bribery, a high rate of industrial accidents, and flagrant violation of the Labour Code.

We are middle-aged people (35-45 years old) with more than a decade of working experience. We have been deprived of work for periods of one to five years. At first we thought that our complaints would find support, if not at local level, then at least in higher institutions and the press.

On the one hand, the Soviet Party and Government call upon citizens to correct violations wherever they occur: in industry and in the life of the state and society. On the other hand, the authorities come down with special brutality on those who respond to propaganda appeals by strictly observing the regulations and speaking out in the interests of the enterprise.

All our attempts to get justice from government authorities have been in vain.

We appealed as individuals to the central organs of Soviet power: the Central Committee of the Communist Party of the

29

Soviet Union, the Presidium of the Supreme Soviet, the Council of Ministers of the USSR, and the All-Union Central Council of Trade Unions. They did not reply to us.

The ruling organs decide our cases only in a one-sided manner: that is, they give bureaucratic answers and transfer us from one department to another. When we appealed to higher authorities, not only did they not take positive measures, but they applied unlawful methods against us for exercising our right of complaint. On the pretext of registering us for an audience with the leadership, they seized us one by one and in groups, sending us to police stations and psychiatric hospitals.

This happens at the highest offices of power: in the Waiting Rooms of the Central Committee of the CPSU, the Presidium of the Supreme Soviet of the USSR and the USSR Procurator's Office.

It is impossible to be received in a single high Soviet institution. All highly-placed personnel — our servants as they like to call themselves — use the police to protect themselves from us.

We decided to unite. We began to act collectively. But just as before, they continued to expel us from Moscow with the help of the police and to put us in psychiatric hospitals.

Collectively we addressed ourselves to all social, Party, council and trade union organisations; to the editorial offices of major newspapers: *Pravda, Izvestia, Trud, Literaturnaya Gazeta*; and to the magazines: *Ogonyok, Kommunist, Partiynaya Zhizn*, and *Sotsialisticheskaya Zakonnost*. [13] We received no reply.

We hoped that the new Constitution of the Soviet Union would rectify the lack of rights enjoyed by the working population. But the evidence of persecution and internment in psychiatric hospitals, which we present in this Appeal, prove that the new Constitution is not taken seriously by Soviet organs, and that it merely serves as a smoke-screen with which to confuse the Soviet people and world opinion.

It was only after we made known these acts of arbitrariness and coercion that we were invited to the *Izvestia* editorial office and to the KGB office. There, we were told, help had been promised.

But all this turned out to be a trick: at the *Izvestia* editorial office, they had only one aim; by taking us in one at a time and humouring us with promises, they tried to induce us to reveal the name of our organiser. They did everything possible to sow discord among us.

30

The KGB organs wanted to find out exactly how many people supported the collective complaint and their addresses, with the ultimate aim of exiling us from Moscow or placing us in psychiatric hospitals.

And so, we decided to organise our own genuinely independent trade union. We did this in order to win the official and legal right to defend our interests — a right guaranteed by the Soviet Constitution — and to enlist in the common struggle for our rights other willing persons whose rights are unjustly violated.

We consider that only through a union of our own, basing itself on the public opinion of workers of all countries, can we force our government to respect the ordinary workers.

In our country, there is no organ which objectively defends the workers' interests. Soviet trade unions do not defend our rights and do not have the necessary authority. For key union posts are held by Communists who did not make the grade in their Party organisations. They are all technicians and engineers who, if not re-elected for a new term, return to their position of dependence on one or other higher management official. And if only for these reasons, they always have to heed the opinions of top management.

Trade-union elections take place in a purely formal manner: the chairmen of trade-union committees are elected and appointed by the management of the enterprise, the Party organiser, and the regional committee of the CPSU. According to the rules, one delegate per ten trade-union members is elected to attend a conference, whose purpose is to hear reports and elect new officials.

It is worth noting that in the Soviet Union there is not one enterprise with less than 100 per cent trade-union membership of the workers and technical-engineering employees.

All of this would be democratic, if only delegates were elected at a general meeting, in the presence of all. However, in order to secure support beforehand, the management and the Party committee resort to the trick of having delegates elected by shop or section. Before this happens, there is a meeting of the technical-engineering personnel at which the trade-union chairman and leaders of the Party committee lay down how the election of delegates should be 'held'.

Afterwards, the elections take place by section or shop. As a rule, the supervisor of the section or shop 'recommends' (i.e.

nominates) whichever candidate he likes. Out of gratitude those he has nominated in turn nominate him and the foremen, as well as someone from the technical-engineering staff. The staff have a separate meeting to elect their own delegates. The workers evidently do not get a look-in. In the end, although workers outnumber staff by ten to one, nearly all those who attend the conference are technical-engineering personnel — that is, those for whom workers' interests are not important.

The workers' delegates receive money which they do not have to return, and the buffets are loaded with normally scarce products and alcoholic drinks.

The management of the enterprise and representatives of the district Party committee, the city trade unions, and the Party organisation are elevated to the presidium without any invitation. These then make a register of candidates, or, in other words, they register on the ballot-paper anyone they like.

No other candidates are registered. That is why the election of the incoming members of the trade-union committee is ensured in advance.

The election of the chairman and the allocation of responsibilities take place at a table laden with food and spirits at public expense, and to the cheers of clinking glasses.

The 'representatives' of the lower trade-union organisations go on to elect territorial trade union committees and so on.

In this *Appeal* we will substantiate our arguments with newspaper items confirming that these are not individual 'shortcomings', but a normal part of everyday life. In its issue of 27 January 1978, *Leninskoye Znamya*[14] carried an article 'Getting used to it' in its general column entitled 'Following the anxious letters':

*'For the second year running, the No.3 Administrative Collective of the Mozhaiskovo Road Building Works has received a flood of anonymous letters to various local and district organisations ... There were similar signs earlier ... On 14 October 1977, there was a trade-union meeting to review the work and hold elections. At the end of this, the workers were given a rouble each, while the office workers went to a restaurant to drink away trade-union money ... The manager of the enterprise, B.F.Stepakin (stated): We have an old tradition; we feel that it is better to drink collectively than to hide in a corner ... The chairman of the trade*

*union committee, N.L.Miroshnikov said: The regional committee of the trade union puts aside special resources for such "gatherings".'*

*Trud* of 20 January 1978 published an article called 'Strange permits' from the town of Yenakiyevo, Donetsk province:

*'The statement of face-worker A.L. Todoseichuk from the platform of the election and review conference is understandable to many at the mine. A.L.Todoseichuk severely criticised the chairman of the mine committee, V.S.Sigarev, for allowing violations of the Labour Code and for the improper allocation of material benefits. The worker produced concrete examples. He said: year after year, the same people enjoy the privilege of spells at health resorts. Worse still: D.Ganzyuk was given a holiday as a reward for absenteeism, and soon after their stay in a drunk-tank[15] E. Litvin and A.Melikhov got permits for one too. And what's this? The managers of the mine — the general director of the Ordzhonikidze Coal Association, N.F.Syomchenko, the secretary of the association's Party committee, V.I.Gromov, and the chairman of the Yenakiyev territorial committee of coal industry trade unions, V.I.Kozlitin, all of whom are on the presidium, let this pass. The reaction was unexpected. A.L.Todoseichuk was a member of the mine committee. Previously he had been recommended for re-election. But when it came to considering the candidates, the presidium did not nominate Todoseichuk. He was not included in the list for secret voting, even though this was proposed from the floor.*

*'Sigarev was again elected chairman of the mine committee, although out of 163 delegates at the conference 59 voted against him. (The authors of the Appeal note that 'according to the rules, a two-thirds majority is required'). In broad daylight, for all to see, the bureaucrats moved to protect Sigarev, disregarding the opinions of those who openly spoke the truth about his improper behaviour....*

*'A.L.Todoseichuk decided to fight for the truth. He wrote letters to the Donetsk regional and republic committees of the coal workers' trade union. He signed it with all his work-titles: face-worker, communist, honoured national miner, holder of the order of the Red Banner of Labour — but no one answered his letters....*

*'Sigarev forges signatures, sells holiday permits to a certain E.A.Sotnikova, who has nothing to do with the mine; as for the*

*head librarian, N.I.Kuzmenko, he simply threw her out of his office (she had come to see him on official business) and the trade-union chairman paid no attention to the official requests of the city procurator. After a short period of time in office, complaints appeared in several departments from Sigarev's subordinates. Each one mentions his rude behaviour to his associates. Because of this, people are leaving "of their own volition".'*

In our previous open letters we wrote: 'there are thousands of similar cases'. Yes, we did not exaggerate. We are convinced that every tenth manual or non-manual worker could fill our ranks.

Let us look at the press. *Pravda* of 21 January 1978 printed an article entitled 'Insufficient persistence': 'At the Petrozavodsk Enterprise No.1126 employing a thousand workers in the town of the same name, one third of the workers left in the last year alone ...'[16]

The newspaper *Vechernaya Moskva* of 21 January 1978, carried an article 'A difficult topic'.[17] Concerning the Sokol'ni-chesky Railwaycar Repair and Building Works in Moscow, we read: 'We pay a great deal of attention to our work with cadres ... What is the result? The balance is not in our favour, as 24 people left while 15 were hired ... '

*Leninist Banner* of 25 January 1978 had an article entitled 'Easy parting': 'Over the past three years 262 workers have left the company. In effect, two out of three left ... '

An article from *Pravda* of 29 March 1976, entitled 'If a labour dispute occurred': 'The legislation of the Armenian SSR, in particular, lays down the penalty for such infringements of the law as breaking a labour contract with a leading worker or removing him from his position of responsibility. However, in our republic there has not yet been cause for the trade union to use this law. Meanwhile, there are occasions when such sanctions have been used ... '

In the same article, not one tenth of the incidents of groundless dismissal of manual and non-manual workers is mentioned; and not one of these received help from the trade unions.

Here is what happened in one large metallurgical factory in the city of Yenakiyevo, Donetsk province, where there are more than 15,000 workers. To whom is their fate entrusted? *Pravda* of 7 January 1978 headlines 'The Effectiveness of Criticism':

*'The Director of the Yenakiyevo Metallurgical Works*

*Yu.T.Cherneta became so offended at criticism in the local paper, that at the beginning of a meeting he put forward an ultimatum: "Either me or her". And he got what he wanted — the meeting did not begin until the "her", the reporter from the paper, left the hall...'*

How do the newspapers write about the creme de la creme, that is, about the Communists? *Pravda* of 21 January 1978:

*'At an enterprise of 1000 workers, 75 are communists... The secretary of the Party committee, A.Min'kovich, recently committed such a misdemeanour that the communists had to elect a new secretary, A.Ul'yanov. The communists hoped that he would take matters in hand. But it did not work out: he didn't have enough character or experience. Furthermore, two other members had to be removed from the bureau: K.Asanov ended up in a drunk-tank, and V.Ushanov was caught out in a fraud....'*

And then 49 workers wrote to *Pravda*: 'the sacking was not discussed in the brigades. There are no noticeable changes at the enterprise....'

The whole country is gripped in a corrosive mould of bureaucratism. This has been witnessed by *us* and by our comrades-in-misfortune, who have grown to over 200: we worked in various enterprises in over 150 different cities and regions of the country.

We are an insignificant fraction of the citizens who everyday crowd the waiting rooms of the central apparatuses....

We ask the ILO and workers' trade unions to recognise our free trade union of working people and to give us moral and material aid.

Yours sincerely,

Members of the new Free Trade Union Association of Working People in the Soviet Union.

[*Signed by the 43 public Free Trade Union Association members*]

## ★ Document 4 / 1 February 1978
### Statute
### of the Free Trade Union Association
### of the Soviet Working People

*Valid from 1 January 1978 to 1 January 1979*

★ Section 1.

*Membership of the Free Trade Union Association of the Soviet Working People*

1. Members of the Free Trade Union Association of the Working People should be manual and non-manual workers whose rights and interests have been illegally flouted by the administrative, soviet, party and judicial organs.

2. A member of the Free Trade Union Association has the right to:

a. freely discuss all the activities of the association, make proposals, openly express his or her views and fight for their opinions until the decision of the Free Trade Union Association is made

b. participate personally in meetings when questions about their own activity or conduct are examined

c. tirelessly carry out the struggle for peace and friendship between peoples

d. raise political consciousness

e. observe the Statute of the Free Trade Union Association

f. participate in the social and political activities of the association.

3. A member of the association is entitled to the following benefits:

a. to receive sound legal aid

b. to receive moral and material aid within the limits of possibility

c. to receive aid in the search for accommodation, and if they are in a position to do so, to give help to their comrades.

4. Enrolment as a member of the Free Trade Union Association is carried out at the request of the person wishing to join, with a preliminary week for consideration in view of the possible consequences of joining.

5. Decisions on the admission of members are made by the assembly.

★ Section 2.

*Organisational structure of the Free Trade Union Association of the Working People*

6. It is organised on the basis of democratic centralism which means:

a. all officials from top to bottom are elected by the members and are accountable to them.

b. all questions concerning the association are decided in accordance with the Statute

c. decisions are made by majority vote.

7. The free and business-like debate on questions of the work of the Free Trade Union Association is a vital principle of internal trade union democracy. On the basis of internal trade union democracy, criticism and self-criticism, activism develops in the membership and practical discipline and political consciousness are strengthened.

8. The Free Trade Union Association is based on the association formed initially by the '43'.

9. The tasks of the Free Trade Union Association are:

a. carrying out obligations incurred by collective agreement

b. recruiting manual and non-manual workers to membership of the Free Trade Union Association.

c. putting into practice the decisions of the association in its defence of rights and search for justice

d. teaching the members of the association to adopt an uncompromising attitude to inadequacies, manifestations of bureaucratism and mystification, bad management and extravagance, and careless attitudes to national property.

★ Section 3.

*Funds of the Free Trade Union Association*

10. The funds of the Free Trade Union Association will consist of:

a. a monthly membership dues and contributions from the unemployed according to their means

b. the dues will be no more than 1 per cent of a worker's wages, but no limit will be set on voluntary donations.

c. contributions by non-members of the Free Trade Union Association in return for the rendering of legal services, the printing and compiling of petitions at rates not exceeding the state tariff

d. material aid received from foreign trade union organisations.

★Section 4.
*On the rights of the Free Trade Union Association as a legal entity*

11. The Free Trade Union Association of the Soviet Working People has a legal character.

As soon as the Free Trade Union Association of the Soviet Working People is recognised by the International Labour Organisation or trade unions of foreign countries, as soon as it receives moral and material support, the Statute will be reviewed in the light of the special situation of working people in our country. The review will be carried out not earlier than one year after the foundation of the Association.

[*Signed by the Council of members of the 43*]

### Vladimir Aleksandrovich Klebanov:
### A Biography

*The founder and moving spirit behind the Free Trade Union Association is Vladimir Klebanov, a mining engineer from the Ukraine. The following account of his life is drawn from his own (unfinished) autobiography, and other documents of the FTUA.* [*18*]

'On 12 September 1968 I was arbitrarily arrested and charged under article 187 of the Criminal Code of the Ukrainian SSR.[19] The grounds of the accusation were as follows: "He has deliberately and systematically spread slanders against the Soviet state and social system in oral and written form ..."

'In reality: since 1958 I have actively spoken out against gross violations of the Labour Code (the implementation of the decree of 1956 about the six-hour working day and the six-day working week). I demanded correct wage payments, and in particular an end to the concealment of industrial injuries in official reports; the correct definition of invalid categories, and proper compensation for miners who suffered injuries through the fault of the management. I demanded the prosecution of the criminals who stole valuable materials, men in important industrial and Soviet positions; an end to bribery, the incorrect allocation of the housing funds and so on.

'From 1958 on the managers of Makeyevka mine and the combine Makeyev-Coal systematically victimised me — they tried to dismiss me several times for no reason, they wrote slanderous reports about me to the KGB — all this they did in the name of the collective.

'In 1959 I was injured in the face ... the management pretended it was an "unlucky accident" and not their fault. Six months later I was no better and had to give up all hope of treatment. I decided to go to court to get compensation for my injury.

'Soon afterwards on the request of the management of the mine and the personal instructions of the First Secretary of the Donetsk Regional Party Organisation, B.Degtyanov, the third category of the disabled [to which Klebanov now belonged] were excluded from the class of invalids.

'Despite the fact that my sight was considerably impaired, I was forced to work underground as a mining foreman. At this time I was also a fourth-year external student at Donetsk Polytechnic, and should have been allocated surface work, but the management refused because of my injury.'

In January 1965 they made a second attempt to get rid of Klebanov on the grounds that the injury was his fault. When this failed 'I was given ten days in which to get out of my flat. The police tried to throw my family and me out on the street, but miners from where I worked prevented this arbitrary act.' On 15 February 1966 the local court ruled that Klebanov belonged 'to a category of workers whose labour disputes about questions of dismissal do not come within the competence of the people's court' (which according to Klebanov was completely untrue).

On 23 December he finally managed to get a decision in his favour after appealing to the Ministry of Mines of the Ukrainian SSR and the Procurator's Office of the USSR.

'For the sake of their egos Degtyanov and Minister Khudosovtsev forced the psychiatrist Sherbin to make a diagnosis of "the history of my illness".' The most he would say was that Klebanov was 'a "querulent" — that is, a litigious person, a malicious gossip.

This was clearly insufficient grounds for refusing me work.' So, they rushed to Moscow and got another psychiatrist, a professor this time, to diagnose Klebanov as having a '"pathological development of the personality" without ever having set eyes on me'. After this, 'attempts to forcibly intern me in a psychiatric hospital for observation, with the help of a whole squad of police, were frustrated by the miners'.

The final verdict of the President of the Town Court of Makeyevka, B.Sitenko, was that:

'"Klebanov has a mental illness which takes the form of paranoia ... This is why Klebanov, as a worker in the mines, has been making complaints since as long ago as 1958, and saying that the management of the mine has been cheating the workers over their pay."'

This was in spite of the fact that the Procurator of the Donetsk region, I.Bashkakov, and the Deputy Head of the Department of Heavy Industry of the Ukraine, I.Nikolayev, had substantiated Klebanov's complaints against the management. Nikolayev wrote on 1 March 1965:

'"Comrade Klebanov informs us that he has appealed to the Party and Soviet organs over a number of years, with the request that they investigate malpractices in the mine — the pilfering of coal and wood, the concealment of cases of industrial injury in the official reports, the violation of the Labour Code, embezzlement from the funds of the enterprise — and bring the guilty to account ... The evidence contained in the letters of comrade Klebanov has been thoroughly checked ... The former head of the mine and others have been brought strictly to account by the Party and the administration for their reported malpractices in the field of production"'

'In reality no measures had been taken'. Most of the men received promotion instead — for example, 'Leshko, the First Secretary of the Regional Party Organisation, became Second Secretary — but of the Central Committee of the Ukraine (now he is Chairman of the Council of Ministers of the Ukraine).'

Klebanov, meanwhile, went on fighting, and on 4 March 1967 got Professor N.Tatarenko to invalidate the diagnosis of paranoia and restore him to the third category of disabled workers: ' ..."the residual appearance of past cranial and cerebral injury, partial atrophy of the left optic nerve ... the recommendation is: he should work as a planner or the head of a club''. But I was only given work as an engineer-planner in September 1967. The rulers of the town of Makeyevka and Donetsk were not prepared to reconcile themselves with this outcome. They fabricated a charge under article 187 of the Criminal Code of the Ukrainian SSR. Hundreds of workers were transferred to other pits, some were made to work in such terrible conditions that they were forced to quit.'

Klebanov was arrested on 12 September 1968 and thrown into Donetsk Prison No.1. In October he was visited by the senior investigator of the Procurator's Office of Makeyevka, Sergeyev, and asked to sign the indictment. When he refused, 'then Sergeyev declared that all this was just a formality. My fate had been decided. I would be taken to the town of Igren for a psychiatric-legal examination, and pronounced mentally ill. I would then be incarcerated in the special hospital of the MVD, to stop me being a bad example to others in the future!

'My family were in a dreadful position. I'd been out of work for about three years. My wife was often ill as a result of childbirth. She didn't work. Our two children had to be fed and clothed. While I was out of work we sold literally everything. Our savings had all gone.

'In protest I started a hunger strike on the first day of my arrest'. On the 27th, 'I was transferred to an isolation cell in the basement. My blanket and mattress cover were removed. There was no glass in the window. It was damp. The cold rose up to my ears. The late September wind blew in.

'On the second day I was beaten ... by a junior lieutenant of the MVD [Ministry of Internal Affairs], who first shackled my hands and feet, then threw me on the ground and began to kick me.'

Lieutenant-Colonel Tsventukh tried to persuade him to eat by installing in his cell a thief who had been on hunger strike for five years. 'He looked terrible. A skeleton ... We see such men only in films about the German concentration camps.' After 20 days Klebanov was shackled and force-fed through a rubber tube which permanently damaged his nose. He finally gave up his hunger strike because 'no-one knew about it'. When he asked why he wasn't getting treatment he was told that he was there 'not for real reasons, but from *higher necessity*, in the interests of social welfare'.

As a result of his continued refusal to admit that he was insane he was transferred to the Dnepropetrovsk special hospital of the MVD on 18 February 1969: 'From the night-time conversations of the orderlies I'd already heard of the MVD special hospital in the Republic as a place one left only "feet first". According to them only those who had committed the most terrible and brutal murders were sent there.' On the way 'first they robbed me. The convoy handed me over to head orderly Bondarenko. I hadn't been able to find my things when I came out of the looney bin. Bondarenko was wearing my sports sweater. Another orderly-thug had my shirt. They were quarrelling over my slippers.' Bondarenko told Klebanov he wouldn't need them any more — 'you won't come out of there alive!'

'The psychiatrist's job was to beat out of my head what was "socially dangerous"; over a number of years and in particular in 1960, I was the instigator of a collective complaint and collected workers' signatures. I took their complaints to the Soviet and Party organs. As a trade union organiser, I came out with criticisms of the management. This was "undermining their authority". This is what they try to cure people of here!'

In hospital, Klebanov didn't stop fighting for one moment — 'I began to petition about my restoration to the invalid category and about a pension for my family. The Procurator of Makeyevka, I.Gaiko; the President of the Court, Sitenko; and Kobzisty, the Head of the Mines and the Combine, told my wife: "We'll give it to you on one condition — agree that your husband is mentally ill.... If you don't do this — it's starvation and total destitution!"'

Finally, in the beginning of September 1970, the Donetsk Regional Court ordered him out to Donetsk Isolation Cell No.1. 'The head of the special hospital of the MVD, Katkov, said: "This is the first time this has happened in all my years of service in the MVD".' After Klebanov still refused to admit in court that he was insane he was transferred from prison to psychiatric hospital and from psychiatric hospital to prison — he spent more than one spell in each of the following — Makeyev Psychiatric Hospital No.1, the Serbsk Institute, and Donetsk, Kharkov and Butynsk prisons. All news of him was lost: 'My wife and children decided that I was dead.'

In June 1972 Klebanov got a decision in his favour 'about the payment of compensation from 11 September 1968 to the present time'. On 7 June 1973 the Supreme Court of the Ukraine ordered his release. This was by no means the end of his troubles. On 26 September 1973 the local court spitefully declared Klebanov 'not responsible for his actions', that is, it took away his civil rights: 'The refusal to allow my family to participate in the elections to the Supreme Soviet of the USSR and of the Ukrainian SSR, had widespread impact on the neighbourhood in Makeyevka — and led the first deputy of the Procurator's Office of the Ukrainian SSR, M.T.Slivayev, to make a personal protest.'

The regional court reversed the decision on 19 April 1974, but it took another six months to get the local authorities to implement it. Meanwhile, the management of the mine refused either to give Klebanov work or to pay him his compensation: 'I am being discriminated against; when I turn for work to my so-called "comrades" they say I'm "mad" ... When I asked to be paid my wages according to the decision of the Council of Ministers of the Ukrainian SSR and the Ukrainian Council of Trade Unions of 28 October 1966 No.1203 — they tell me "you're healthy".'

'The director of the Khoronzhy mine told me on 6 May 1974, "it's impossible to give you work at the mine since there are no vacant posts. Besides, we are reducing the number of engineers and technicians in the mine". Not one enterprise will have me because they've written in my labour book "Dismissed in connection with arrest" ... This is a glaring infraction of the Labour Code. One needs proof of release — I haven't got it. My requests for rehabilitation or removal of the endorsement from the labour book receive no reply.'

*Klebanov's biography unfortunately breaks off at this point and we have no more information about him until 1977. By this time he had taken his petitions to Moscow. There his incredible endurance and determination made him the obvious leader of the dissatisfied group of complainants.*

On 10 February 1977 Klebanov was arrested together with V.S.Cheverov by 'KGB agents who tried to charge me with the bombing of the Moscow Metro'.[20] At the police station 'a tame psychiatrist was waiting' and he was held in Moscow Psychiatric Hospital No.7 and in Donetsk Psychiatric Hospital for two months. 'At the same time agents of the KGB and the Makeyevka Procurator's Office ransacked his flat, as well as T.I.Volkova's, V.V.Chetverikov's and Z.T.Klebanov's, without a procurator's

43

warrant.' In these searches 'I have lost 2,100 roubles from the money I had received in partial compensation for my unjustified detention in the Dnepropetrovsk Special Psychiatric Hospital.' Meanwhile the investigation of his complaints 'was discontinued on the instructions of the Procurator's Office of the USSR'.

'On 19 December 1977, V.A.Klebanov, V.V.Chetverikova, and V.F. Luchkov were seized by the agents of the Donetsk KGB and Police Station No.108 (led by KGB Captain V.S.Pakhomov and Police Captain Kochetkov) despite the protest of more than forty comrades of Klebanov, Chetverikova and Luchkov and a crowd of angry Muscovites. All this took place at the main entrance of the Chief Telegraph Office in Gorky Street. They were taken to Police Station No.108 and there insulted by the Chief of Police, Lieut.-Col. Zubkov.

'Klebanov was forcibly transported to the Psychiatric Hospital No.7. On 22 December 1977, the agents of the Donetsk KGB transferred him to Donetsk Regional Psychiatric Hospital No.1. There, in order to justify the arbitrary actions of the Donetsk KGB agencies, he was diagnosed as having "a paranoiac development of the personality" and as being a champion of "justice".

'Chetverikova and Luchkov were ordered to sign undertakings that they would leave Moscow within 72 hours.'

On 21 December 1977, 17 members of the Free Trade Union Association signed a collective protest on Klebanov's behalf. They insist that: 'The behaviour of V.A.Klebanov does not bear a socially dangerous character', and they

'DEMAND:

'1. The release of Vladimir Aleksandrovich Klebanov, illegally and arbitrarily hospitalised in Psychiatric Hospital No.7.

'2. We demand from the medical workers of Psychiatric Hospital No.7 and its head doctor M.S. Rubashov, strict observance of the instruction on immediate hospitalisation, No 06-k4-43, of the Ministry of Health USSR.

'3. That notice be taken of the collective petition of 7 November 1977, signed by 43 people and addressed to you, and that you take steps to further the solution of the problems outlined in the collective petition.'

They succeeded in obtaining his release, but 'at 1 p.m. on 27 January 1978 another attempt was made to seize Klebanov, Chetverikova and Luchkov... while they were walking along

Gorky Street in Moscow' and force them 'to go to a nearby police station without a Procurator's warrant or even any kind of explanation ... This time KGB captain V.S.Pakhomov's "operation" fell through' — the balance of forces was such that 'in the fight which followed their comrades managed with the help of passers-by to protect them from the arbitrary violence unleashed by so-called defenders of law and order'. However, on 7 February 1978 Vladimir Klebanov was again detained in Moscow, and once more taken to the Donetsk Psychiatric Hospital where he was put into 'strict isolation'. The latest report is that he 'was transferred by early May 1978 from a psychiatric hospital in Donetsk to a prison. If confirmed this might indicate that charges are being brought against Klebanov.'[21]

## Members of the Free Trade Union Association of Soviet Working People

★ Case histories
FTUA status, occupation and place of residence

1. Bobryshev, Ivan Petrovich:
FTUA candidate member. Welder. Susuman, Magadan Region, RSFSR. Twice seized by Moscow KGB agents and has been held in Psychiatric Hospital No.7 since 1 May 1977.

2. Boiko, Aleksandr Mikhailovich:
Candidate member. Miner. Donetsk, Ukrainian SSR. In January 1977 he was placed in Psychiatric Hospital No.7 on the orders of the Supreme Soviet of the USSR. A veteran of the Great Patriotic War [second world war], he was sacaked two years before he was due to retire.

3. Dvoretskaya, Mariya Ivanovna:
Member. Worker in the factory Dzetisu (in Russian 'Seven Waters.'). Alma-Ata, Kazakhstan SSR.

4. Dvoretsky, Fyodor Pavlovich (Mariya's husband):
Candidate member. Compressor operator.

Mariya writes: 'I appeal to international opinion to help me, a semi-literate woman, to obtain the release of Fyodor Pavlovich Dvoretsky, my husband and the father of our three children, who was shut up in the Special Psychiatric Hospital No.2 of the MVD [Ministry of Internal Affairs] on 6 May 1977. He is being held in a special psychiatric hospital because while he was working as a compressor operator in the Il'insky district, together with workers at the creamery and later at the shoe factory, he signed a protest to the Society for the Protection of Public Property against thefts and fraudulent wage payments to non-existent workers.

'He was tried secretly without witnesses. Although I was present at the court, they would not allow me to defend him. The psychiatrist V.T.Lomakina ruled him to be not responsible for his actions and socially dangerous and recommended that he be isolated in the MVD Special Psychiatric Hospital at the prison in Alma-Ata. Nothing more has been heard of him. This is partly because all this happened so far from Moscow.

5. Dyatlov, Fyodor Fydorovich:
Candidate member. Worker. Makeyevska, Ukrainian SSR.

'Born in 1959, he was arrested at the hotel "Rossiya" in February 1977 on suspicion of arson.'[23]

6. Fufayeva, Anna Sergeyevna:
Member. Etcher at the Fryazinsky 50th Anniversary factory. Ogudnevo village. Shchyolkovsky district. Moscow region.

Fufayeva, mother of two children, was sacked from her job on the orders of Kolgomorov, the director of the factory 'because she had openly criticised the administration which had over several years made wage payments incorrectly for work done in harmful conditions'. Her attempts to get her job back were foiled by Kolgomorov. He persuaded 'a doctor who was in direct dependence' on him to write a report stating that 'A.S.Fufayeva is not fit to work at her speciality and has refused other jobs'. On the basis of this, Judge Zalogin of the Shchyolkovsky District Court 'took the management's side' and decided against her. 'In reality, the more authoritative Erisman Institute has stated that A.S.Fufayeva is capable of working as an etcher.' Legally 'the management had no right to sack her' because 'through the fault of the administration she had suffered an industrial injury and is in receipt of a semi-invalid benefit'.

Persecution of all kinds followed her attempts to uphold her rights in the courts: 'In order to intimidate A.S.Fufayeva and to undermine her reputation among the workers, they put her in jail for ten days, ostensibly for hooliganism and drunkenness. In reality she has worked for 30 years and has received government awards for exemplary and conscientious work. After threats she was obliged to leave her room in the town and take refuge in the village of Ogudnevo. But even there she has no peace. On the initiative of the President of the village council, V.M.Fufayev [an unfortunate coincidence of names — eds.], the plot of land she rents is being ruined.'

When she took her case to the capital 'G.Marshalkin, an official of the Moscow Committee of the CPSU, faced with the truth about years of persecution and procrastination, tries to shield those who break our socialist laws'.

7. Gaidar, Nadezhda Ivanovna:
Member. Engineer, Kiev, Ukrainian SSR.

On 6 May 1976 Gaidar went 'to the reception room at the Central Committee of the CPSU, where she saw the Deputy Receptionist V.I.Filatov. He sent her on to Tsibulnikov, the Deputy Receptionist of the USSR Procurator's Office. She turned up twice at the times indicated by Tsibulnikov. The second time she was seized by police officers, taken to Police Station No.108 in Moscow and then taken to Psychiatric Hospital No.13. There they began at once to give her injections of the drug aminazin. The head of Ward 2 of Psychiatric Hospital No.13, L.I.Fyodorova, said regarding N.Gaidar's hospitalisation: "We will not make any diagnosis of her. We have made a note that she is suffering from nervous exhaustion brought on by her quests for justice. To keep her from complaining any more we will keep her here for a while and then we will send her to Kiev via a special detention point. There too they will hold her for a while". When Gaidar's acquaintance V.A.Klebanov came to ask after her and to say that her two children had been left without their mother and without anyone to look after them, Dr Fyodorova told him: "Then next time she'll think a little before going to complain." N.Gaidar was transferred from Moscow to a psychiatric hospital in Kiev, from which she was released after two months.'

In February 1978 members of the workers' group said that they had appealed collectively on behalf of Nadezhda Gaidar in 1975. It appears that already in 1975 she herself was among the workers who were acting collectively, and since then she has been an active participant of the group.[24]

8. Galimova, Slu Abdugalimova:
Candidate member. Headmistress. Ufa, Bashkir ASSR.

'I have been out of work for five years and am being systematically persecuted by the police, supposedly for parasitism. The Ufa City Court decided in my favour but the Ufa Education Authority leadership keep trying to get a review of the case, in the Supreme Court of the Bashkir Autonomous SSR.

'I have come to the conclusion that Soviet laws are directed against and operate only against the working people in the interests of the bureaucracy. From the age of 13, since the first days of the war, I have laboured for the good of my country, without holidays or days off. I never expected that in my declining years I would find myself unemployed. There is no-one to whom I can complain, and to do so would be futile. There is nothing left but to commit suicide and end it all.'

9. Gudz, Mikhail Stepanovich:
Candidate member. Trawler-man. Zaporozh'ya Ukrainian SSR.

Member of CPSU. 'Shut up in Psychiatric Hospital No.7 in March 1977. Sacked after a quarrel with the captain of the trawler.'

10. Gur'yev, Mikhail Yegorovich:
Member. Foreman at Rostov-Energy Metal Works. Krasny Sulin, Rostov Region, RSFSR.

'I worked on repairs at the factory (PRP) Rostov-Energy in Rostov on Don. I was the leader of a brigade of metal workers and a shop foreman, but after I criticised the administration I was forced to go away to work as a metal worker in the 6th salary grade.[25] This was not enough for the administration; they started a persecution campaign against me, i.e. they transferred me to other, unskilled jobs, thus reducing my wages; they wouldn't pay me extra for night work, so I was obliged to refuse this work. They tried to compel the workers to vote to dismiss me, supposedly for absenteeism — they tried to pass off the days and nights I missed when I refused to do unskilled work as absences from work. The workers refused to vote.

'They were always threatening me, "leave the works, we'll still get you". They carried out their threat — I was illegally dismissed in 1976. As a result of the stress I got backache. An attempt was made on my life — they wouldn't investigate it. I have given 20 years, the best years of my life, to the energy industry. I have 14 incentive awards and decorations, I have the medal for "outstanding work". I have appealed to all the official organs and I have received in return either formal rejections or from some institutions *no reply at all*.'

Of his subsequent history we know that on 12 July 1977 he together with N.P. Ivanov, M.L. Melenteyev and V.I.Kucherenko was dragged from the Waiting Room of the Central Committee of the CPSU to Moscow Police Station No.46 and forced to sign a statement 'that they would never again appear in the Waiting Room of the CC-CPSU'.

'One evening in January 1978, the police forced their way into his flat and searched it; Gur'yev was in Moscow. They explained their behaviour to his terrified wife and children by saying that they'd received urgent instructions to place M.E.Gur'yev in a psychiatric hospital. They departed with threats.'

11. Isayevy (husband and wife):
Kuibyshev, RSFSR.

Both are over 60. They were seized in the Procurator's Office in February 1977 and 'placed in Psychiatric Hospital No.7 where Isayeva had a serious heart attack'.

12. Ivanov, Nikolay Pavlovich:
Member. Bulldozer driver at the Sokolov-Sarbay Ore-Processing Combine 1958-76. Rudnyi, Kazakhstan SSR.

'I was persecuted by the management because in 1974 I tried to get the proper wage for my work as laid down in Soviet law. The management transferred me to lower paid work for no reason at all and illegally deprived me of bonuses; reprimanded me for refusing to carry out lower paid work without the proper transfer order specified in the labour laws.

'In contravention of the provisions of the Labour Code about dismissal procedure, I was sacked in 1976 for malicious infraction of labour discipline, although I had been working there for 18 years and no-one had ever made any complaint about me. During these years, as a result of working in bad conditions, I had contracted an occupational disease. It was incurable, and the management did not have the right to throw a sick man like me onto the street, leaving my family without a means of livelihood. My health is getting worse. My attempts to obtain justice from the Soviet bureaucrats only worsen my already desperate situation.'

He was later arrested together with four other members of the

Free Trade Union (Konstantin Gucherenko, Valentin Poplavsky, and Viktor Luchkov) for being in Moscow without official permission [see case history of Gur'yev].

13. Izvekova, Valentina Nikitichna:
Member. A secretary at the Executive Committee of the Chernigov Soviet. Chernigov, Ukrainian SSR.

'[I was] sacked in 1975 for exposing the Executive Committee Chairman I.N.Shmakov. I.N.Shmakov had been abusing his official position for ten years. In violation of the established procedure he made decisions on the allocation of state and co-operative flats, with self-interested motives, and accepted bribes. He used his official position to induce his colleagues V.G.Trush, L.N.Tkach and L.L.Solomatina to have sex with him (as was established by the Judicial Collegium of the Chernigov Regional Court). In the cause of truth I spent four months in prison, leaving my two young children without a mother, and to this day I have no work.

'The crook Shmakov lay in the prison hospital for three months and was rehabilitated by the Supreme Court. After his release, he was immediately found a management job although he has no education, only his Party card.

'On 28 July 1977, the Deputy Head of the Waiting Room of the Procurator's Office of the USSR tried to persuade me to betray my comrades, the signatories of a collective complaint to L.I. Brezhnev of 20 May 1977, promising in return to obtain an interview for me with the First Deputy of the Procurator General of the USSR, A.M. Rekunkov, and to "reconsider" my case.'

14. Kategorenko, Taisiya Andreyevna:
Member. Painter in the housing department of the Podol'sk Ferro-Concrete and Building Material Works. Klimovsk, Moscow region.

'My persecution began when I denounced the managers of the works for pilfering and illegal allocation of housing space.' After this she was 'three times sacked and three times reinstated'. The managers persuaded the Podol'sk court to order her (illegal) eviction 'in her absence the Klim police threw the contents of her flat out into the rain ... Some of her belongings were lost, others were ruined'. She tried to obtain justice but 'my complaints are not examined and I get formal replies full of lies. They are constantly trying to intimidate me, by saying that they will put me in prison as a "parasite", and they won't investigate the matter properly. I have been unemployed since 1975.' The latest news we have of her is that 'On the night of 16 January 1978 N.A.Agapov, Head of the Klim police, and his men forced their way into her flat: T.A.Kategorenko's son, Gennady, and the neighbours showed them the door. Agapov left threatening, "We'll put you in prison or the other place ..." (i.e. the psychiatric hospital).'

15. Kochetov, Anatoly Mikhailovich:
Candidate member. Disabled worker. Moscow.

'Seized in the Presidium of the Supreme Soviet of the USSR, while petitioning about a flat problem in February 1977.'

16. Korchagin, Viktor Ivanovich:
Candidate member. Engineer, leader of a brigade of fitters. Kamerovo, RSFSR.

'I was a member of the CPSU for ten years, but as a sign of protest I handed in an application to leave the CPSU.' Six months later, on 17 January 1977 he was 'seized in the exit of the offices of the Central Committee of the CPSU and detained in Psychiatric Hospital No.7. He is now being held in the psychiatric hospital in his home town of Kemerov. *He was mentally healthy.*'

17. Kozlova, Yelena Petrovna:
Candidate member. Skilled engineer. Registered in Voronezh, RSFSR (in fact homeless).

'Her failure to obtain reinstatement at work and the restoration of her rights reduced her to a plight so desperate that she was driven, on a visit to Lenin's tomb, to place her petition on the sarcophagus. She was forcibly removed by agents of the KGB and men from Police Station No.80 to Psychiatric Hospital No.3 ("Sailors' Rest") and kept in Ward 6 for the violent. She was released on 28 June 1977. She is mentally healthy. She has asked for the termination of her Soviet citizenship.'

18. Kozlova, Klavdiya Aleksandrovna:
Member. Smelting furnace worker at the Lipetsk Iron and Steel Works. Lipetsk, RSFSR.

'In 1975 I was illegally dismissed for criticising the management over bad working conditions. In order to justify my sacking the management thought up the story that I had worked as a steam engine driver and been dismissed because of my poor eyesight. In June 1976, I had an interview with the Deputy Procurator General of the USSR, A.S.Pankratov. He did not even hear me out and insulted my honour as a worker, calling me a speculator. Several months later the Deputy Chairman of the RSFSR Supreme Court, Sergeyeva, nevertheless registered a protest. But the Lipetsk People's Court, in collusion with the management of the works, declared that we had reached an amicable agreement, that is, I had agreed to accept payment for 3 months of enforced absence from work. This was a filthy lie, and I am refusing to start work again because they owe me money for all the years I have been deprived of work. I have had to sell almost everything that I had managed to scrape together in the course of 20 years' work.'

'On the night of 26 December 1977 Lipetsk police agents forced an entry to her flat and tried to take her to a psychiatric hospital. She was saved from these tyrants by her relatives and neighbours.'

19. Krasovsky, M.N.
Bobruisk, Belorussian SSR.

'On 21 October 1977 ... he was dragged from the Procurator's Office of the USSR to Moscow Police Station No.108 where "he had a talk with the psychiatrist". Earlier in the month Krasovsky had been taken to Moscow Police Stations No.166 and No.64 after he'd asked for an appointment with the leadership of the Procuracy of the USSR.'

20. Kravchenko, Tat'yana Ivanovna:
Member. Engineer-economist. Nikolayev, Ukrainian SSR.

'Citizens are detained en masse in psychiatric hospitals in the town of Nikolayev ... including Anastasiya Mefodiyevna Nosyryova, Maria Mikhailovna Kharichkova, Nadezhda Yeromeyevna Bondarets and Tat'yana Ivanovna Kravchenko' who signed the open letter of 7 November 1977, and was seized at home on 26 December and 'put into a psychiatric hospital and held there for three months. She was released on the demand of 76 citizens who knew her well after repeated letters to the Central Committee of the CPSU and the national press.'

21. Kucherenko, Varvara Ivanovna:
Member. Points operator in a curing and pickling plant. Makhach-kala, Daghestan ASSR.

'The administration and trade-union committee of the plant wanted to get rid of me because I had exposed them for stealing goods. Therefore, hoping I would leave work of my own free will, they transferred me to another job with lower pay, although according to the law a manager of a section does not have the right to do this without the worker's agreement.

'I appealed to the Procurator's Office of the USSR and to the courts of the Daghestan ASSR, but there they failed to look into my complaint properly. Seeing that I was getting no support from anywhere, the administration sacked me, ostensibly for absenteeism. This allegation did not correspond to the facts, since I had not refused to work but simply wasn't going to work for next to nothing! I went to the Waiting Room of the Procurator's Office of the USSR. Procurator A.S.Budersky refused to put me down for an interview and had me dragged to the police station where by dint of threat on 8 July 1977 they forced me to give an undertaking to leave Moscow, although I had committed no anti-social or hooliganist acts but had only given my documents in to the Central Committee of the CPSU.

'On 8, 12 and 22 July 1977 I sent the editors of *Pravda* complaints (signed by five and seven witnesses) against my having been dragged illegally to the police station, but to this day, I have received no reply.'

On 22 June 1977 she was grabbed in the Building of Marxism-Leninism on Gorky Street. They tried to put her into a psychiatric hospital, but the psychiatrist refused to hospitalise her. She was taken to Special Detention Unit No.2 of the UVD [Administration of Internal Affairs] of Moscow City Executive Committee. The chief of the Special Detention Unit No.2, Senior Lieutenant P.V.Yefimov illegally held Kucherenko in a prison cell and ordered that she be taken under guard to the cuty of Ryazan although Kucherenko came from Makhachkala.

When she complained about this the MVD [Ministry of Internal Affairs] replied on 16 December 1977 'the fact of violation of legality on the part of the police has not been established'. The Procurator's Office decided 'the decision of the judges about the refusal to reinstate you is correct and your protests against it are rejected' (26 December 1977). Kucherenko understandably concludes 'I was sacked on 26 December 1972 and no-one in our "beloved" country cares a fig for me or the fact that I have been left without a livelihood.' [See case history of Gur'yev]

22. Kuvakin, Vsevolod D.
The Free Trade Union Association's lawyer. Moscow.
He was dismissed from his job as labour law inspector of the

Central Council of Trade Unions of the Oil and Gas Industries and 'barred from the profession' on 20 October 1977. The reason was that in 1976-77 he wrote letters to the Central Committee of the CPSU, the Politburo, Brezhnev, and the Presidium of the Supreme Soviet in which 'I expounded my views on the internal policies carried out in the USSR and criticised various aspects of the internal policies of the Soviet government and party'. In a statement in February 1978 he wrote: 'I bring to the notice of the international press that I have been illegally dismissed from my job for political reasons and that this happened within the apparatus of the central trade union body, "which stands guard over the worker's right to work".'

In an appeal to the Administrative Council of the International Labour Organisation in Geneva on 10 March 1978 Kuvakin points out that: 'According to the legislation of the USSR, every able-bodied citizen is obliged to work (and, as is said in article 60 of the Constitution of the USSR, "in his chosen socially useful occupation"). A citizen who does not work for over four months can be called to account by the administration and in some cases prosecuted. I have been unemployed for almost five months already and in spite of all my appeals requesting that I be given a job, I have not been offered work in my field. I get the impression that I am being deliberately denied the chance of work, so that I can be accused of evading socially-useful labour and be prosecuted.'

23. Levit, Yakov Matusovich:
Candidate member. Assistant newspaper editor. Odessa, Ukrainian SSR.

A veteran, decorated in the second world war, and member of the CPSU. On 16 April 1975 he and his daughter, an 'Intourist' interpreter, 'were seized in the Waiting Room of the Central Committee of the CPSU, when, in front of the eyes of hundreds of citizens from various cities across the country, one complainant, driven to despair, committed suicide. The same day dozens of exasperated citizens were arrested or kicked out of Moscow'.

24. Luchkov, Viktor F.
Member. Miner. Donetsk.

On 22 October 1977 V.F. Luchkov 'was taken under escort from the Procurator's Office of the USSR to Police Station No.108 after he asked for an audience with the leadership of the Procuracy of the USSR'. He rang up the offices of *Izvestia* with his story and on 2 January 1978 he received the following reply: 'Questions connected with reinstatement at work are decided by the court. It is possible to appeal against the court decision in a higher court and in the Procurator's Office. This does not fall within the competence of the editorial board'.

25. Makarov, Mikhail Vasil'yevich:
Candidate member. Engineer. Moscow.

Unjustly dismissed, unemployed for five years. On 19 June 1977 he was promised an appointment with the First Deputy of the Procurator-General of the USSR. He was then removed forcibly to Police Station No.108 and from there to Psychiatric Hospital No.3, where he was detained for several days. On 14 November 1977, he was arrested in the Waiting Room of the Central Committee of the CPSU, and taken to Police Station No.46. The psychiatrist they had called in refused to hospitalise Makarov. His case has not been settled.

26. Manokova, Tamara Mikhailovna:
Member. Accountant at the 'Rose Valley' holiday camp in Sudak. Sudak, Crimea region, Ukrainian SSR.

'I insisted that effective measures should be taken against the men responsible for financial irregularities. In retaliation I was sacked from my job four times, starting from 11 July 1973. The director of the holiday camp, Trofimov, was dismissed because of the irregularities which I'd brought to light, but I'm still being held terrorised and sacked without reason. How many times can they do this — after all, there's a limit to what a person's nerves can stand.

'Instead of defending me and investigating the shady practices of the camp administration and the management of the factory which runs it (the Belaya Kalitva aircraft factory, Rostov Region), the Deputy General Procurator of the USSR, A.S.Pankratov, called me a speculator and threatened to have me imprisoned. It is very strange: they tell us we must fight against crime, but in reality they punish honest men.'

27. Matyusheva, Natal'ya Semyonovna:
Member. Formerly a waitress in the 'Storm Petrel' Hotel run by the Gorky Trade Union Council. At present a mechanic. Gorky, RSFSR.

'I was sacked supposedly for absenteeism. In fact what happened was that I had been working in the "Storm Petrel" hotel since 1970, first as a maid and then when I'd got my qualifications, as a mechanic. My character will not let me tolerate injustice. And when a motor mechanic called Morov died at work because the doctor, Dr N.B.Yevich, refused to treat him, I spoke my mind about his inhuman behaviour. From that time on she [the doctor] started a persecution campaign against me. Instead of calling Dr N.B.Yevich to account, the management and the Trade Union Committee took her side, and terrorised me in all sorts of ways. I was showered with false accusations of indiscipline and was forced to take my case to Moscow, since both the People's Court of the city of Gorky, and the Collegium for Civil Cases of the Gorky Regional court took the side of the management. In Moscow, too, I failed to get justice. When I was still a girl I volunteered for the front line. I have been awarded state decorations.'

28. Melent'yev, Mikhail Leonidovich:
Member. Driver at the Alma-Ata Public Transport Maintenance Works, Depot No.7. Alma-Ata, Kazakhstan SSR.

'For five years I was an example to the collective — a member of the shock troops of communist labour. I had twenty years' working experience. I refused to participate in the squandering and theft of materials ... Because of this the management became prejudiced against me.

'In 1974 I had an operation after which I was supposed to be given light work. Instead I was assigned the strenuous jobs, for which, what is more, I received 50 roubles a month less than for the work I did before. I complained to the management and to the trade union. I didn't get an answer. Instead, the management set drunks and thugs on me to beat me up.

'A false document was drawn up according to which I was supposed to have been drunk on the job and I was sacked on this pretext. In fact I never touch drink and no-one has ever made any complaints about me. Not one of the protests I made to Soviet and Party bodies and to the People's Court has been properly investigated.

'Thieves stick together, and as if that wasn't enough one member of the Regional Party Committee said to me: "Why don't you bugger off to America!"' [See case history of Gur'yev]

29. Melent'yeva, Mariya Petrovna:
Member. Furnace worker in Brick Factory No.1 of the Alma-Ata Building Materials Combine. Alma-Ata, Kazakhstan SSR.

'Firing bricks ... is heavy, dirty work and according to Soviet law I ought to be given an early pension, i.e. at the age of 50. Wherever I turn, no-one will give me a straight answer, and instead they send me 20-year-old documents. As a matter of fact, there already exists a list (No.2, 22 November 1972, Ref.71289) according to which a brick furnace worker working with solid fuel is entitled to an early pension, i.e. at the age of 50. It is basically not a woman's job. I have worked 27 years at the firm. If I tried to get justice, like my husband I would be thrown out on the street too and we would be left without our livelihood. So I continue to suffer, sick as I am and worn out by many years of heavy work. I have to put up with insults from the Trade Union Chairman, Sokolov, whose duty is to watch over and defend the workers. I have been awarded state decorations but no-one takes any notice of me.'

30. Murav'yov, Pyotr Mikhailovich:
Leader of a brigade of roofers.[26] Leningrad, RSFSR.

Aged 70, 'he has been held in the special hospitals of the MVD in Leningrad, Sychyovk, and Dnepropetrovsk. At the present time he is in Psychiatric Hospital No.1 in the city of Donetsk, as his son, a member of the CPSU, does not want to take responsibility for him. He has been held for 18 years, because in 1959 he sent a petition to Khrushchev with a photograph of himself with his cap held in his outstretched hand, begging for compensation for his groundless dismissal and imprisonment.'

31. Nikitenko, Vasily Nikolayevich:
Candidate member. Surgeon. Klim, Moscow region.

'In 1971 his situation became so desperate that he tried to enter the American Embassy with his wife and two young children'.[27] After this KGB agents interned him in the Serbsk Institute. He was held there for about seven months. Then the court ruled that he was socially dangerous and sent him for a compulsory 'cure' to the Special Psychiatric Hospital of the MVD in Kazan. He was held there until 1975. He is still persecuted, and out of work. His wife, a psychologist, was held in the Kashchenko Psychiatric Hospital No.1, and their two children in a children's home for their solidarity with him.

32. Nikitin, Vasily Yurevich:
Candidate member. Mining engineer. Donetsk, Ukrainian SSR.

'He was held in the Dnepropetrovsk Special Psychiatric Hospital of the MVD attached to Prison No.1 for having exposed abuses at a mine in the Donbass. In March 1977, he tried to enter the American Embassy to make the way he's been treated publicly known, was arrested, interned in Psychiatric Hospital No.7 and then transferred to the Donetsk Regional Psychiatric Hospital No.1, where he is still being unjustly held'.

33. Nikolayev, Yevgeny Borisovich:
Member. Biologist (he graduated from Moscow University in 1969 and then worked for four years at the All-Union Institute of Scientific and Technical Information and for one year at the Institute of Disinfection and Sterilization; he also specialises in foreign languages). Moscow.

Unlike most members of the unofficial trade union group, Nikolayev had been active as a dissenter for a number of years and has been the subject of a number of samizdat reports over the past eight years. In 1970 he was dismissed from his research job after refusing to 'take on extra work in honour of the 24th Congress of the CPSU'. He was hospitalised four times during 1970-4, because, as his psychiatrist told him: 'his views of society' represented 'a social danger'.[28]

The first thing we know about this intellectual's involvement with the workers' group is that 'Divisional Inspector of Moscow Police Station No.137, Pulayev, steadily terrorised Y.B.Nikolayev and his family. Pulayev and other policemen from station No.137 made attempts to arrest Nikolayev without a procurator's warrant on 31 January and 1 February 1976 and 13 January and 29 January 1977 and in May 1977. On 4 October 1977 Nikolayev was illegally detained in the city of Petropavlovsk-Kamchatsky along with I.E. Gavrilov, a resident of the city, and sentenced to 15 days.'

In late November 1977 the first press conference of the workers' group was held in Nikolayev's flat. Subsequently, on 12 December 1977, a police officer came to visit Nikolayev and said that 'he had a warrant calling for Nikolayev to be given "urgent medical assistance". Nikolayev refused to admit the police officer to his flat and the latter said that "all the same he would catch Nikolayev somewhere on the street".' Throughout the winter of 1977-78 Nikolayev's flat formed the centre of the group's activities.

He was detained on 15 February 1978 and confined in Moscow Psychiatric Hospital No.1. In mid-April, a British psychiatrist tried to visit him in hospital but was refused admission on the grounds that 'Soviet law prevented foreign doctors from examining patients receiving treatment' (no such law exists). The psychiatrist publicly reported that Nikolayev's wife was not allowed to see him because 'she has been mixing with the wrong people'. He was also told by friends of Nikolayev that he had been treated 'with a drug which made him apathetic'.

34. Oganesyan, Shagen Akopovich:
Member. Engineer. Yerevan, Armenian SSR.

'I worked at the enterprise Armenergonaladka in the city of Yerevan in the job of senior engineer. A conflict developed between myself and the Party organs. They trod my citizen's right underfoot by refusing to give me a work record thus preventing me from accepting an invitation to travel to Poland.[29]

'My appeals to higher Party organs to solve the conflict on its merits only infuriated the management at my place of work and led them to create a situation unfavourable for normal work. I then appealed to the courts for a resolution of the labour conflict that had arisen. The courts took the side of the management of Armenergonaladka. The biased nature of the investigation of my complaints conducted by the higher Party organs, including the Central Committee of the CPSU, had the consequence that I was forced to protest to the 25th Congress of the CPSU.

'As a result of all my fruitless appeals, I was obliged to leave work on 12 January 1976 and appeal personally to the Central Organs. My quest for the restoration of my dignity and the defence of my honour had the consequence that, to cap everything, I also became unemployed.'

35. Otrokhova, Alisa Zakharovna:
Candidate member. Manager of a shop. Voroshilovgrad, Ukrainian SSR.

'They came to her flat in the night and tried to drag her to a psychiatric hospital, on her return from a personal interview with the Procurator General of the USSR, comrade R.A. Rudenko.'

36. Ovchinnikova, Alina and Diana Dmitriyevna (sisters):
Alina is an accountant, Diana a post-office worker. Minsk, Belorussian SSR.

'Since January 1972 our aged mother M.V.Ovchinnikova has been deprived of her residence registration for Minsk and even the court refuses to recognise her as a member of her daughters' families. Having thus reduced the official number of people in our flat from five to four, in December 1973 they threw us out of our third room and forcibly installed a third family. The aim of this was that the new family would make slanderous reports on us which would enable the Ministry of Communications of the Belorussian Republic to drive us out of our flat in the town centre. (The block is on its books as it claims administrative rights over it.) This family has been promised a flat in return for its "services".

'Our families are crowded into a spare room much smaller than the health laws allow. Living conditions in the flat (which has a shared kitchen) are unendurable and make it quite impossible for three families to get on together.

'When she complained to the Government, A.D.Ovchinnikova was slandered at her place of work (the Ministry of Communications BZVTs plant) and in the Minsk press. She was then thrown out on to the street and her family (herself, her mother and her grown-up daughter) completely broken up. Police threats that she would be imprisoned for a year for living in the flat and for daring to complain caused serious damage to her health. By July 1966 A.D.Ovchinnikova was left with no alternative but to take her complaints to Moscow despite her poor state of health. For this "absenteeism" she was given the sack. Threats forced D.D. Ovchinnikova, who worked at the Head Post Office, and her widowed mother, to leave their jobs "of their own volition".

'At present neither of us has work. We have been forced to defend the weaker members of our families, ourselves and our property against police thuggery and attempts at the forcible resettlement of all five of us into a separate flat on the strength of a document listing only three names. No-one will clear up the matter locally. They are letting us slowly starve, ruthlessly waiting for us to die, since we have all been deprived of our health and our means of livelihood.' (See case history of Ryakhina)

37. Poplavsky, Valentin Tikhonovich:
Member. Department head at a ferro-concrete plant. Klimovsk, Moscow Region.

One of the most active members of the group. He was sacked in 1975 for 'exposing the abuses of the factory director V. Polstyanov ... On Polstyanov's instructions I was beaten up by Klimovsk police officers in my own flat in front of my wife, children and 100 year old father. After my appeal to the CPSU Central Committee on 30 June 1976 I was arrested for no reason by men from the Moscow KGB and Police Station No.46 and after an hour's trial sentenced to 15 days in jail.'

At 7p.m. on 10 February 1977 the Divisional Inspector and a KGB officer 'burst into my flat and tried to arrest me again' but 'the people wouldn't let them do it'. Poplavsky suspected that 'They probably wanted to hang the Metro Business on me too', as they did with Vladimir Klebanov (see note 20).

'On 16 October 1977 Podol'sk policemen dragged L.Poplavskaya (his wife) and V.T.Poplavsky to the police station at 6am on Sunday supposedly to arrange jobs for them. On 3 November 1977 the Deputy Chief of the Klimovsk police, A.A.Vorontsev and Divisional Inspector Subbotin again summoned the Poplavsky couple to the police station and threatened to take Poplavsky to court for parasitism.

'On 5 January 1978 at 6 o'clock in the morning, a police squad forced their way into Poplavsky's flat; the squad consisted of N.A.Agapov, chief of the Klimovsk police, his deputy A.A. Vorontsov, Divisional Inspectors Biketov, Syomin and Dostoyevsky, and three other policemen. They dragged him by force to the Police Station, and from there to the Podol'sk Psychoneurological Outpatients Department No.17. The psychiatrist Yatsynenko pronounced him mentally healthy, refused to bow to the insistent request of the overbearing guardians of the law and order for Poplavsky's hospitalisation.' On 18 May 1977 the police got their way and Poplavsky 'was sentenced to one year imprisonment on charges of "parasitism".'

38. Reznichenko, Pyotr Fyodorovich:
Member. Metal worker on a poultry farm. Odessa Region, Ukrainian SSR.

The following letter was sent to the Politburo of the CPSU and various state bodies, signed by 21 people, on 27 January 1978: 'On 21 January 1978 at 7.30p.m. Pyotr Fyodorovich Reznichenko, resident of Odessa oblast, who had striven along with us to get justice on the question of his unjust dismissal from his job as a metal-worker at a poultry factory, was arbitrarily arrested at the Kiev railway station.

'P.F.Reznichenko was held for 24 hours in a cell in the Kiev railway station.[30] On 22 January 1978 he was conveyed to the Moscow City Central Committee's special detention centre but was not accepted there.

'On 23 January 1978 at 6 p.m. P.F.Reznichenko was again conveyed to the Moscow City Central Committee's special detention centre and is being held in cell no.7. They tried to charge him with malicious petitioning and violation of the passport law from 1 January 1977.

'The treatment of comrade Pyotr Fydorovich Reznichenko is in direct violation of Article 54 of the Constitution of the USSR: "Citizens of the USSR are guaranteed inviolability of the person. No-one may be arrested except by a court decision or on the warrant of a procurator." The police had no such warrant.'

Twenty members of the Association of Free Trade Unions signed a similar 'Appeal to International Opinion' on Reznichenko's behalf.[31]

39. Ryakhina, Zinaida Grigor'yevna:
Member. Teacher. Village of Orto-Say Alamedsky district, Frunze region, Kirghiz SSR.

Seized together with A.D. Ovchinnikova 'while walking along a street in Moscow and held in Special Reception Room No.1 of the UVD [Bureau of Internal Affairs] where on the orders of its chief, I.A.Podlesny, they were stripped naked, degradingly searched, Ryakhina's coat was even torn. Then they were kicked out of Moscow.

40. Shcherbakov, Valentin Vasil'yevich:
Candidate member. Worker at a copper smelting combine. Karatash, Chelyabinsk Region, RSFSR.

'On 17 February 1976 he was seized by men from Police Station No.46 after visiting the Waiting Room of the Central Committee of the CPSU. He was forcibly consigned to the Kashchenko Psychiatric Hospital No.1 and from there conveyed under guard to the "Birgil'da" Psychiatric Hospital No.2 in Chelyabinsk, where he was unjustly held until 30 September 1976.

'On 14 April 1977 he was seized a second time by the police in a railway station. This time they placed him in Psychiatric Hospital No.13, from where he was transferred back to Chelyabinsk Psychiatric Hospital No.2. In early January 1978 Valentin V. Shcherbakov disappeared, and it has to be presumed that he has again been placed in a psychiatric hospital.'

41. Shkorbatov, Yakov Aleksandrovich:
Member. Night watchman. Village of Belozersky, Krasnodarsky Kray, RSFSR.

'I was educated as an ichthyologist [scientist specialising in the study of fish]. I was wounded in the war and cannot obtain work in my field and so I work as a watchman for 60 roubles a month.[32] I have no housing either and live in a railway carriage which used to be lived in by prisoners.' They had water, heating and electricity, but Shkorbatov, 'a decent, honest man', hasn't. His quarrels with the authorities began 'on 29 December 1976, on my way to work, I was knocked down by a police car driven by a drunken policeman, N.Yemel'yanov, and his drinking companion Police Sergeant M.T.Achkov. The Procurator of the Dinsk District of Krasnodar stopped work on the case because the drunks who caused the accident were officers of the Krasnodar police'. Shkorbatov was in hospital for two months but 'I received not a kopek in compensation. My complaints are ignored'.

42. Shipilevoy, Pyotr Timofeyevich:
Candidate member. Metal worker for the Kiev Water Supply Company. Kiev, Ukrainian SSR.

He was reported 'held in the Serbski and Dnepropetrovsk special hospitals of the MVD for standing in Red Square in Moscow with a placard calling for the proper observance of the Constitution'.

43. Travkina, Vera Logvinovna:
Member. Recently working as a newspaper seller in the 'Soyuzpechat' kiosk in Kiev. Kiev, Ukrainian SSR.

'I was unjustly dismissed. I appealed to the courts and the Procurator's Office of the USSR and of the CC of the CPSU. Our leaders are hiding from the people behind the KGB and the police. I took part in the Great Patriotic War and was a lieutenant in the medical corps, helping wounded Soviet soldiers. I have been awarded state decorations. Now when I'm on the threshold of ruin, I cannot get help anywhere, and people won't even give me a decent hearing. It makes me sick when I hear how free and well-off we are supposed to be!'

44. Tsado, Larissa Ivanovna:
Candidate member. Accountant. Stepnoy, Kazakhstan SSR.

She was arrested in May and 'at the main telegraph office at the end of June 1977, and had a "discussion" with a psychiatrist.'

45. Tsvyrko, Gennady Aleksandrovich:
Member. Minsk, Belorussian SSR.

'On 13 January 1978 he was promised an appointment with the First Deputy of the Procurator-General A.M.Rekunkov. On the orders of the chief official in the Waiting Room of the Procurator's Office of the USSR, N.V.Tsybul'nik, Tsvyrko was taken under guard to Police Station No.108. There he was held in Special Detention Room No.1 until he signed an undertaking that he would leave Moscow "of his own free will" and "never come back again to complain". He was also charged with violating internal passport regulations, although on the day of his arrest Tsvyrko was living in a hotel. Tsvyrko was conveyed back to Minsk. Earlier, on 5 October 1977, Tsvyrko was committed to the violent ward of the Kashchenko Psychiatric Hospital No.1 on the orders of the officials of the Procurator's Office of the USSR, and held there for about ten days.'

46. Tullikov, Kuz'ma Gavrilovich:
Candidate member. Pensioner on the Lenin State Farm. Irtysky District, Pavlodarsk Region, Kazakhstan SSR.

'Invalid of the First Class, veteran of the Great Patriotic War [second world war], has been awarded state decorations. He was detained in Psychiatric Hospital No.7 after he asked for an increase in his pension.'

47. Usitskov, Anatoly Fyodorovich:
Candidate member. Worker. Leningrad, RSFSR.

Born 1924. 'He was refused residence registration everywhere because he had come out of prison.' He placed his complaint on Lenin's coffin and as a result 'was twice detained in Moscow psychiatric Hospital No.7 — on 20 December 1976 and 15 January 1977'.

48. Yan'kov, Gavril Timofeyevich:
Member. Freight handler and trolley driver in Shop No.14 of the Moskabel factory in Moscow.

'I was sacked in November 1975 for criticising the factory management. At first they assigned me to heavier work, but that meant less pay. I complained that this was unjust. So they took savage reprisals against me. They sacked me for refusing to work.

'In February 1977 Divisional Police Inspector Shatrov burst into my flat with three KGB officers and made a thorough search of it. They predicted that I would be thrown out of Moscow within the month.

'On 23 May 1977 they again broke into my flat, and in my absence threw my belongings into the street. Then they took them away — I don't know where to. Shatrov stole my documents — my passport and labour book. On 27 May they returned my passport with my registration struck out and ordered me to go wherever I liked, but out of Moscow. I got my labour book back only on 14 June 1977.

'Since 27 May 1977 I have been sleeping in railway stations. They took to arresting me and taking me to the police cells in the Kursk station. At first they would keep me for an hour or two. In Moscow Police Station No.26 they kept me locked up with thieves and hooligans for over a day. Then they photographed me in three poses. They made me have a "discussion" with a psychiatrist. Nobody bothers the criminal and drunkards who roam Moscow's streets, but I, an honest man who had lived in Moscow for many years, have to leave.'

According to Free Trade Union sources: 'In December 1977, Yan'kov was arrested in a railway station without a procurator's warrant and was held in the Special Detention Unit of the Moscow City Executive Committee. On 2 January he was first tied up on directions of the psychiatrist on duty, then thrown into a cell in the hope of causing a psychosis, and forcibly placed into Psychiatric Hospital No.3, "Sailors' Rest", where he was held until 16 January 1978, and as the psychiatrists explained to us, he was "treated for a cold in his head". In actual fact, they were trying to persuade him to become "mentally ill" promising him Moscow residence in return. He was released only on our demand.'

Twenty-one FTUA members appealed on behalf of Yan'kov, Reznichenko, Tsvyrko and others to the Chairman of the KGB, Yu.V.Andropov and to the Ministry of Internal Affairs. They wrote: 'The repression directed against us at the very historical moment when the new Constitution of the USSR is being introduced into the country, obliges us to predict that the Constitution may not be to every worker's taste.

'We demand an end to groundless persecution for exercising the right of complaint.

'The guilty must be called to account.

'We present this document to international opinion.

*'There are over two hundred of us in all.*

27 January 1978'

[This wasn't the end of Yan'kov's troubles — according to the latest reports (April 1978) he is now in prison.]

49. Yaschenko, Mariya Ivanovna:
Candidate member, Worker. Nikolayev, Ukrainian SSR.

'In September 1975, 54 citizens of Nikolayev — Komsomol

and Party members — appealed to the General Procurator of the USSR to protect M.I. Yashchenko from persecution by those who were trying to put her in a psychiatric hospital. The petition was left unanswered. On 13 January 1976, they renewed their appeal, turning to the 25th Congress of the CPSU with the request that an answer be sent to Mariya Mikhailovna Matusevich. There has been no answer to this day.'

## Other known members of the Free Trade Union Association of Soviet Working People

★Their FTUA status, occupation, place of residence, and any known history

1. Anason, Nikolay Arkad'yevich:
Candidate member. Worker, Minsk, Belorussian SSR.

2. Antonova, Klara Petrovna:
Candidate member. Engineer. Kiev, Ukrainian SSR.

3. Arutyunyan, Genrikh Sarkisyanovich:
Candidate member. White collar worker. Moscow, RSFSR.

4. Bakhereva, Nina Andreyevna:
Member. Occupation unknown. Sverdlovsk, RSFSR (Siberia).

5. Balanyuk, Viktor Matveyevich:
Candidate member. Bricklayer. Odessa, Ukrainian SSR. Had a spell in Dnepropetrovsk special hospital.

6. Baletskaya, Vera Anatol'yevna:
Candidate member. Worker. Makeyevka, Ukrainian SSR.

7. Barcho, Medzhid Kazbuletovich:
Candidate member. Worker. Krasnodarsky Kray, RSFSR (far east).

8. Barchugov, Aleksandr Petrovich:
Member. Occupation unknown. Leningrad, RSFSR.

9. Beketov, Nikolay Ivanovich:
Candidate member. Worker. Krasnodarsky Kray, RSFSR.

10. Beletskaya, Dina Alekseyevna:
Candidate member. Worker. Nikolayev, Ukrainian SSR.

11. Bilechenko, Nikolay Makarovich:

Candidate member. Engineer. Frunze, Kirghiz SSR.

12. Bobryshev, Ivan Petrovich:
Candidate member. Welder. Susuman, RSFSR (far east). One of the 35 listed as having been in prison or psychiatric hospital in Document 1.

13. Boletsky, Vasily Anatol'yevich:
Candidate member. Worker. Nakayevka, Ukrainian SSR.

14. Bondarets, Nadezhda Yeremeyevna:
Candidate member. Worker. Nikolayev, Ukrainian SSR. Detained in Nikolayev Psychiatric Hospital.

15. Bortsova, Yelena:
Candidat member. White collar worker. Pevek, RSFSR (far east).

16. Cherkasov, Mikhail Dmitrevich:
Candidate member. Miner. Makeyevka, Ukrainian SSR.

17. Chernikova, Nadezhda Illarionovna:
Candidate member. Teacher. Stavrapol, RSFSR (North Caucasus). Has been in prison or psychiatric hospital.

18. Chernyak, Yekaterina Ivanovna:
Candidate member. Worker. Chernigov, Ukrainian SSR.

19. Chetverikova, Valentina Vasil'yevna:
Member. Unknown. Makeyevka, Ukrainian SSR. Secretary of the FTUA. Klebanov's wife.

20. Cheverov, Vitaly Sergeyevich:
Candidate member. White collar worker. Moscow. Arrested with Klebanov on 10 February 1978.

21. Davydova, Lidiya Mikhailovna:
Candidate member. White collar worker. Moscow.

22. Davydova, Natal'ya Dmitrevna:
Candidate member. Insurance agent. Komi ASSR.

23. Dzharov, Shamil Mamedovich:
Member. Occupation and place of residence unknown.

24. Estova, Lyudmila Tikhovna:
Candidate member. Worker. Klimovsk, Moscow Region.

25. Faizin, Rif Amirovich:
Member. Occupation unknown. Kalinin. RSFSR.

26 Fazylkhanov, Mamed Mamedovich:
Candidate member. Welder, Kazan, RSFSR. Spent two weeks in Psychiatric Hospital No.7.

27. Filippov. Leonid Ivanovich:
Candidate member. Miner. Makeyevka, Ukrainian SSR.

28. Gavrilenko, Viktor Mikhailovich:
History teacher. L'vov, Ukrainian SSR. Is in the special hospital in Dnepropetrovsk.

29. Garagan, Grigory Iosofovich:
Candidate member. Worker. Kaliningrad, Moscow Region. Had a spell in the Kashchenko Psychiatric Hospital No.1 in Moscow.

30. Gavrilov, Ivan Yegorovich:
Candidate member. White collar worker. Petropavlovsk-Kamchatsky, RSFSR (far east). Detained with Y.B.Nikolayev (see case history above).

31 Gladun, Tat'yana Gavrilovna:
Candidate member. Worker. Nikolayev, Ukrainian SSR.

32. Golovochuk, Gatal'ya Vasil'yevna:
Candidate member. White collar worker. Donetsk, Ukrainian SSR.

33. Gucherenko, Konstantin:
Status unknown. Railway worker. Caucasus.

34. Gulisaryan, Arshalius Khachaturovna:
Candidate member. Disabled worker. Sukhumi, Georgian SSR.

35. Gunchenko, Anatoly Tarasovich:
Candidate member. Worker. Nikolayev, Ukrainian SSR.

36. Ignat'yeva, Galina Mikhailovna:
Member. Occupation unknown. Fergana, Uzbek SSR.

37. Ionkin (first names unknown):
War invalid. Voronezh, RSFSR. The Ministry of Social Security put him in hospital in 1977.

38. Ivanovna, Marina Mikhailovna:
Candidate member. Worker. Moscow.

39. Kharichkova, Mariya Mikhailovna:
Candidate member. Pensioner. Nikolayev, Ukrainian SSR. Detained in Nikolayev Psychiatric Hospital.

40. Kimayeva, Anna Aleksandrovna:
Candidate member. Accountant for the restaurants of Sverdlovsk. Sverdlovsk, RSFSR (Siberia). Had a spell in the Meshchersky Psychiatric Hospital.

41. Klebanova, Zinaida Trofimova:
Member. Unknown. Makeyevka, Ukrainian SSR.

42. Koponeva, Klavdiya Vasil'yevna:
Candidate member. Nurse. Makeyevka, Ukrainian SSR.

43. Kosterin, Roman Moiseyevich:

Candidate member. Photographer. Sovetsk, RSFSR. Has been in prison or psychiatric hospital (Document 1).

44. Kosterina, Ignessa Prokof'yevna:
Candidate member. Teacher. Sovetsk. Wife of above.

45. Kostylov, Oleg Borisovich:
Candidate member. Worker. Nikolayev, Ukrainian SSR.

46. Kosygin, Fyodor Mikhailovich:
Candidate member. Miner. Makeyevka-West, Ukrainain SSR.

47. Kovalenko, Vladimir Stepanovich:
Candidate member. Miner. Makeyevka-West, Ukrainian SSR.

48. Kozyrov, Zavrek Alekseyevich:
Member. Unknown. Unknown.

49. Kryuchkov, Nikolay Nikolayevich:
Candidate member. White collar worker. Moscow. Has been in prison or psychiatric hospital (Document 1).

50. Kurakina, Nadezhda Vasil'yevna:
Member. Occupation unknown. Volgograd, RSFSR. Had a spell in psychiatric hospital.

51. Kutakhin, Ivan Stepanovich:
Candidate member. Worker. Klimovsk, Moscow Region.

52. Kuznetsova, Tat'yana Sergeyevna:
Candidate member. Worker. Vladivostok, RSFSR (far east).

53. Lilenko, Nadezhda Kirilovna Aleksandriya:
Candidate member. Worker. Kirovgrad Region, Ukrainian SSR.

54. Namedov, Sabir Ivanovich:
Candidate member. White collar worker. Berdyansk, Ukrainian SSR.

55. Masalov, Vasily Ivanovich:
Candidate member. Worker. Mozhaisk, Moscow Region.

56. Maslov, Eduard Konstantinovich:
Status unknown. Teacher of Engineering. Ozharel, Moscow Region. Was kept in a Moscow psychiatric hospital.

57. Matushevich, Mariya Mikhailovna:
White collar worker. Nikolayev, Ukrainian SSR.

58. Mazurovskaya, Nina Artomovna:
Candidate member. Worker. Nikolayev, Ukrainian SSR.

59. Medvedev, Yury Ivanovich:
Candidate member. Engineer. Moscow.

60. Meiyer, Vera Eduardovna:
Candidate member. Worker. Tula Region, RSFSR.

61. Mikhailova, Aleksandra Grigorevna:
Member. Occupation unknown. Novgorod.

62. Moskvina, Anna Vasil'yevna:
Candidate member. White collar worker. Lvov, Ukrainian SSR.

63. Murav'yov, Nikolay Grigor'yevich:
Candidate member. Deputy head doctor. Taganrog, Rostov
Region, RSFSR. Has been in prison or psychiatric hospital.

64. Nechiporchuk, Vera Terent'yevna:
Candidate member. Accountant. Odessa, Ukrainian SSR.

65. Nosyrova, Anastasiya Mefodiyevna:
Candidate member. Worker. Nikolayev, Ukrainian SSR. Detained
in Nikolayev Psychiatric Hospital.

66. Obshitosh, Krestina Ivanovna:
Candidate member. Worker on a collective farm. Zakarpatsky
Region.

67. Ossi, Zhanna:
Candidate member. White collar worker. Kokhta-Yarve, Estonian
SSR.

68. Ostaf'yev, Sergey Vasil'yevich:
Candidate member. Pensioner. Donetsk, Ukrainian SSR. Held in
early 1977 in Moscow Psychiatric Hospitals Nos. 13 and 7.

69. Ostrevnaya, Vera Vasil'yevna:
Candidate member. White collar worker. Krasnodarsky Kray,
RSFSR (far east).

70. Pashkovskaya, Liliya Ignat'yevna:
Candidate member. Nurse. Donetsk, Ukrainian SSR.

71. Pavlova, Tat'yana Ivanovna:
Candidate member. Jurist. Khabarovsk, RSFSR (far east).

72. Pelekh, Valetina Alekseyovna:
Member. Occupation and place of residence unknown.

73. Petrosyan, Eduard Petrosovich:
Candidate member. Engineer (research worker). Leningrad,
RSFSR.

74. Pogrebnyak, Nadezhda Lavrent'yevna:
Candidate member. Worker on a collective farm. Inozemtsevo,
Stavropol'sky Kray, RSFSR.

75. Polyanskaya, Valentina Pavlovna:
Candidate member. White collar worker. Saratov, RSFSR.

76. Popko, Stanislav:
Candidate member. Worker. Petrad, Latvian SSR.

77. Popov, Ivan Ivanovich:
Candidate member. Pensioner (aged 75, former regional secretary of the CPSU). Dnepropetrovsk, Ukrainian SSR. Has been held in the Dnepropetrovsk special hospital.

78. Poznyakov, Anatoly Nikoronovich:
Member. Worker. Moscow.

79. Pryadko, Grigory Mikhailovich:
Candidate member. Worker. Village of Zoltnise, Poltava Region, Ukrainian SSR.

80. Red'ko, Mariya Nikolayevna:
Candidate member. Worker. Votaisk, Rostov Region, RSFSR.

81. Rekovskaya, Larisa Viktorovna:
Candidate member. Employee. Issyk, Alma-Atinsk Region, Kazakhstan SSR.

82. Savinkov, Aleksandr Mikhailovich:
Candidate member. Miner. Makeyevka, Ukrainian SSR. Has been in prison or psychiatric hospital (Document 1).

83. Sergiyenko, Yevpotiya Logivna:
Candidate member. Worker on a Collective Farm. Village of Bel'tsovo Primorsky Kray.

84. Shapochkina, Valentina Alekseyevna:
Candidate member. Worker. Valdivostok, RSFSR (far east).

85. Sharifulina, Natisa Abdurakhamanovna:
Candidate member. Worker. Ufa, Bashkir SSR.

86. Shestakov, Fyodor Ivanovich:
Member. Occupation unknown. Saratov, RSFSR.

87. Shestakova, Yekaterina Tikhovna:
Candidate member. Occupation unknown. Saratov, RSFSR. Wife of the above.

88. Sidorova, Anna Stepanovna:
Candidate member. Cleaner in a bakery. Pestovo, Novgorod Region, RSFSR. Three months in Psychiatric Hospital No.13.

89. Soroka, Yelena Moiseyevna:
Worker on a collective farm. Lidekhova, Ternopol Region, Ukrainian SSR. Held in psychiatric hospitals on three separate occasions.

90. Stenkin, Ivan Ivanovich:
Candidate member. Driver. Moscow. Attempt to hospitalise him, 3 November 1977.

91. Sukhanova, Lidiya Ivanovna:

No personal details known.

92. Taran, Yelena Alekseyevna:
Candidate member. Worker. Vinnitsa, Ukrainian SSR. Attempt to hospitalise her, 22 July 1977.

93. Teiler, Nelli:
Candidate member. Housewife. Issyk, Kazakhstan SSR.

94. Tolyshkin, Aleksandr Aleksandrovich:
Candidate member. Worker. Lipetsk, RSFSR.

95. Trishkin, Nikolay Ivanovich:
Candidate member. White collar worker. Podol'sk, Moscow Region.

96. Tsvetkova, Nina Mikhailovna:
Candidate member. White collar worker. Kiev, Ukrainian SSR.

97. Valedo, Liliya Artemovna:
Member. Occupation and place of residence unknown.

98. Vats, Anna Moiseyevna:
Candidate member. Worker on a collective farm. Perenyaten Roven Region, Ukrainian SSR. Detained three times in Moscow psychiatric hospitals.

99. Volkova, T.I.:
Makeyevka, Ukrainian SSR. Flat raided by KGB at time of Klebanov's arrest in February 1977.

100. Yakovenko, Viktor Ivanovich:
Candidate member. Worker. Moscow.

101. Yershova, Natal'ya Ivanovna:
Candidate member. Worker. Kutaisi, Georgian SSR.

102. Zakharov, Aleksandr Vasil'yevich:
Candidate member. Worker. Moscow.

103. Zakharova, Klavdiya Tikhonova:
Candidate member. Occupation unknown. Moscow. Wife of the above.

104. Zaochnaya, Tat'yana Karpovna:
Member. Occupation unknonw. Moscow.

105. Zasimov, Dmitry Yakovich:
Status unknown. Manager of a shop. Yuzhno-Sakhalinsk, RSFSR (far east). Was held in Psychiatric Hospital No.7.

106. Zhuraviov, Nikolay Pavlovich:
Candidate member. Doctor. Uch-Kuduk, Uzbek SSR.

107. Zotova, Lyudmila Tikhovna:
Candidate member. Worker. Klimovsk, Moscow Region.

# 2:

# The Right to Strike
## Introduction

Strikes are becoming more frequent in the Soviet Union. As Holubenko, the only person to have made a detailed study of the subject, says: 'The working class, terrorised into passivity under Stalin, is slowly recovering its strength.' There is a general anger, a feeling that things aren't fair. But this anger isn't as yet directed against the regime, just against certain aspects of it. These strikes are 'skirmishes in the unfolding class struggle'.[1]

Most strikes take place in peripheral regions, not in the big cities. This is because these areas suffer more from the shortage of goods, and are less easily penetrated by the secret police. This is especially true of the non-Russian republics; and as strikes there pose a less serious threat, the government pays less attention to discontent among the workers.

The biggest and most widespread explosion of working-class discontent occurred in 1962. Nothing on a similar scale has happened since then. The big price increases in meat and dairy products announced on 1 June 1962 were greeted with fury everywhere. There were sit-down strikes, mass protest demonstrations on factory premises, street demonstrations, and, in several cities, large-scale rioting. We know of turmoil in Grosny, Krasnodar, Donetsk, Yaroslav, Zhdanov, Gorky, and even Moscow.

By far the most violent outbreak of struggles occurred in the Donbass region, and in particular in the city of Novocherkassk. The strike in Novocherkassk (described below) is remarkable for the speed with which it spread from the locomotive works to the town; for the fact that the solidarity action in the town was led by *women* (textile workers); and for the extreme violence with which it was repressed. It was a lesson that, in spite of the official blanket of silence, has resounded throughout the Soviet working class. (Fifteen years later Valentin Ivanov was told by his work-mates in

73

Kuibyshev, over 1,000 miles away, that demonstrating wouldn't get anywhere: 'If the whole town protests — they'll simply mow us down with machine guns as they did in Novocherkassk in 1962.'[2])

Most important of all was the fact that the strike in Novocherkassk was only one of many in the region. One account even says that a regional strike committee was formed to co-ordinate the protest: 'the insurgents in the Donbass region reportedly considered ... the demonstrations in Novocherkassk unsuccessful because they rebelled there without the consent of the strike organisation offices in Rostov (on Don), Lugansk, Taganrog, and other cities. This would confirm rumours and reports concerning a headquarters for organised opposition in the Donbass and also explain that a co-ordinated demonstration didn't develop because of tumult breaking out over the price increases before final preparations could be made.'[3] If true, this is a fact of overwhelming importance.

This frightened the authorities, and Khrushchev's successors initially allowed wages to rise. There was thus a lull in working class activity until 1969 when Brezhnev and Co. returned to Khrushchev's policy of low wages. Since then strikes have become more frequent. They are sparked off by three main issues: low wages, in particular a sudden drop in bonuses or piece-rates due to the management readjusting the norms; shortages of food and consumer goods; and inadequate housing. Police brutality is often the last straw.

Leonid Plyushch, the exiled Ukrainian dissident and marxist, gives information about a riot that occurred in 1967 in Priuluk, a town of under 100,000 in the Chernigov region of the Ukraine: 'The police arrested one worker who worked in a factory in Priuluk and beat him severely. The worker died as a result of this beating. After several days the workers from the factory where the murdered man had been employed were going to bury him. The procession filed past the same police station where the murder occurred. Several women shouted: "Down with the Soviet SS men!" The crowd hurled itself upon the police building, smashed everything in the building and beat up the policemen. Workers from other factories came out to join them. A small army division was sent against them but the workers drove them away. The workers got together and wrote a letter to the Central Committee of the Party in which they demanded that the guilty be given up for a lynching, that five men who were arrested after the workers' protests be freed and that all Party and Soviet administrators in the town be sacked. They stated that if the army was sent against them they would set fire to the petrol pipe-line which passes through the town. After some time a general arrived from Moscow and promised to carry out all the workers' demands. He stated only that the government could not allow a lynch trial and that the murderers would be punished by judicial means. 'What happened further I don't know.'[4] Another such 'disturbance' occurred in the last week of June 1972 in Brezhnev's home town of Dneprodzherzinsk, a centre of heavy industry in the southern Ukraine. A recent samizdat document provides a detailed account of the events which led to the ransacking of the local police station by an angry mob. Two policemen and eight civilians died.[5]

Strikes over wages sometimes succeed if they occur in centres of extreme strategic importance. Thus in May 1973 the workers at the Kiev machine-building factory went on strike for higher pay. A member of the Ukrainian Politburo flew in immediately. The dispute started at 11a.m. and by 3p.m. they'd won and the management had been sacked.[6]

Because of police repression against strikes, Soviet workers only engage in them under extreme conditions. According to Vadim Belotserkovsky, a former Soviet industrial journalist of ten years standing and now in exile, because of the fear of repression strikes tend to occur spontaneously:

'But a more common variant is the so-called "Italian strike", in which workers turn up to the factory but in practice do no work. I know about this tactic both from my own experience and from samizdat. As a rule, once a strike breaks out, the workers' demands are satisfied. But for that very reason, they are soon followed by repression against the organisers. And since most workers live in the provinces, they lack one vital means of defence — access to world opinion through contact with foreign correspondents. So strike organisers often simply disappear into mental hospitals without a trial, or else provocateurs are used in order to charge them with assault or hooliganism.'[7]

The most famous example of a dispute over bad housing is the strike at the hydro-electric station in Vyshgorod, just outside Kiev, in mid-May 1969. It was remarkable for the high level of organisation — all the workers in the settlement joined in. They marched under banners carrying such slogans as 'All Power to the Soviets'. They sent a delegation to Moscow with a petition signed by about 600 workers. Like many such petitioners, their leader Hryshchuk was arrested and disappeared.[8] This didn't stop them from writing more petitions (see Document 2 below).

The most violent and well-publicised outbreaks have occurred in the Ukraine, which for nationalist and economic reasons is the most politically conscious part of the USSR. However, the strike movement is by no means confined to the Ukraine.

## Revolt in Novocherkassk

### ★ Document 1 / May 1977
### Never to be Forgotten[9]

On 3 May 1977 *Pravda* published an article entitled 'Shooting on Liberty Square'. It stated 'About 200 policemen suddenly appeared in Haymarket Square. They fired on the strikers. Cut down by the volleys of bullets, *people fell and died on the street*. This took place 91 years ago in Chicago in the United States of America. It happened on 1 May ...

'Soldiers and policemen rushed into Liberty Square. They began to shoot at the demonstrators — workers, peasants and students. Cut down by the volleys of bullets, *people fell and died on the street*. This took place the day before yesterday in San Salvador, in one of America's dependencies — the Republic of El Salvador. This happened on 1 May'.

Now let us tear outselves away from this *Pravda* article and focus on a city which is much closer to us. A large peaceful demonstration flows through the streets of Novocherkassk. Above the columns of people fly red flags, a portrait of Lenin, and banners bearing peaceful slogans. It looks like a May Day demonstration. But it's not. It is a popular protest.

The day before, the Soviet government had doubled the price of meat and dairy products. At the same time, at the largest factory in the town (the electric locomotive works) piece-rates were cut by 30 per cent. This was too much for the workers. They called a strike and they and their families came out on the street.

When the demonstrators reached the square in the centre of the town, their path was blocked by infantry and tanks. There was a long pause. Then the machine-guns rattled. They fired straight at the demonstrators — men, women and children. Struck by *dum-dum* bullets, *people fell and died on the street* — at the foot of the Lenin monument and all around it in the huge square and adjacent streets. This happened fifteen years ago, on 2 June 1962, in a country which calls itself *socialist*.

The crushing of this workers' protest was directed by members of the Central Committee of the CPSU, under the leadership of two members of the Politburo — Frol Kozlovy and Anastas Mikoyan. The job of carrying out the massacre was given to General Pliev, commander of the North Caucasian Military District and Basov, first secretary of the Rostov CPSU. And they performed this task 'brilliantly'.

The long pause on the square was due to the fact that the soldiers from the local garrison refused to fire on the unarmed people. General Pliev quickly replaced them with soldiers of non-Russian nationality from other parts of the district. And these carried out the task. After they'd done this black deed, they too were replaced. It's not good for you to stay and gaze at peaceful, unarmed people you have killed and maimed! Another advantage was that the new lot of troops could be given cartridges without dum-dum bullets. This allowed the authorities to claim later that the slaughter on the streets of the town must have been committed by enemy agents since the Soviet army didn't have any guns which used dum-dum bullets.

Neither *Pravda* nor any other Soviet newspaper printed a single word about the Novocherkassk events. The authorities took measures to stop any news getting out of the town, and to snuff out talk inside it.

Novocherkassk was surrounded by the army. No-one was allowed in or out of the town. Indiscriminate arrests and searches were made, according to a secret list of names. The dead and the wounded were carted away. And to this day nothing is known of what happened to one or the other. The families of the dead and wounded were moved to distant towns [i.e. Siberia]. A series of trials took place. Two of them were open (entry by ticket). At one of the trials nine men were sentenced to death and two women given 15 years each.

People were so terrorised and intimidated, that if it had not been for the persistent, courageous work of Alexander Solzhenitsyn, who little by little gathered information about the Novocherkassk events, the world would not have known anything about them to this day. Even now we don't know eactly how many people died — only that 70 to 80 corpses were left on the square. How many of the wounded died or were finished off later, how many were shot after trial, is still a secret.

These deaths must never be forgotten or forgiven!

We call for the day of 2 June to be a day of commemoration for the victims of despotism, a day of struggle against the bloody official terror!

[Signed by 85 members and supporters of the Moscow, Ukranian and Lithuanian Helsinki monitoring groups]

Two Further Accounts

*Two other detailed accounts give us additional information about the Novocherkassk events. They are written by people from completely different backgrounds. The first is John Kolasky, who as a member of the Canadian Communist Party was sent to the USSR on a Party scholarship to study in Kiev for two years at the Higher Party School.* [10] *The second is Alexander Solzhenitsyn, a former inmate of a labour camp and a bitter anti-communist.* [11] *Both agree, however, on the ferociousness with which the workers were repressed.*

Kolasky writes that the news of the piece rate reductions 'had the effect of an electric shock on workers who were already dissatisfied with their miserable living conditions and a hopelessly inadequate diet.

'A group of employees from one of the shops sent a delegation to the management to protest against the lowering of the rates. No-one would meet them. This increased the tension and more people began to gather from other shops. A train, passing on a railway that ran in the vicinity, was stopped. Someone began sounding the locomotive whistle and then the factory sirens. The mood of the crowd was ugly.

'Soon the militia arrived but was driven off. Then soldiers appeared in armoured cars followed by tanks and occupied the shops. The crowd did not disperse, but increased as employees of the new shifts arrived. (The shops worked on a three-shift system.) The following morning several thousand workers, who had remained at the locomotive works all night, began to march on Novocherkassk, which is located on a tributary of the Don River. In order to enter the town they had to cross a bridge which was blocked by soldiers.

'In the meantime another mass of people had already gathered in the central square of the city before the building of the local committee of the Party, which was guarded by a formation of the KGB armed with automatic weapons. The city secretary of the Party appeared and began to address the crowd. Some tried to shout him down; others hurled objects at him. Suddenly the KGB detachment opened fire into the crowd. Shooting also began from other directions. In one area, when soldiers were ordered to fire one officer pulled out his Party membership card, tore it up, and then shot himself. Many soldiers refused to obey the command.

'According to reports, at least several hundred were killed. Martial law and a curfew were imposed, troops and tanks patrolled the streets and the area was completely sealed off so that no one could either leave or enter. This was accompanied by house to house visits of the KGB agents, mass arrests and secret trials.'

In *The Gulag Archipelago* Solzhenitsyn gives us details of his research. He sees the strike in Novocherkassk as 'a turning point in the modern history of Russia' — the first open rebellion against Soviet rule since the time of the Civil War.

The strike began on 1 June in the forge and foundry of the locomotive works. Horror at the sudden plunge in their living standards led to a spontaneous mass meeting, a quite extraordinary event: 'Kurochkin, the works manager arrived. When the workers asked him "What are we going to live on now?" this well-fed parasite answered: "you're used to guzzling meat pies — put jam in them instead". He and his retinue barely escaped being torn to pieces.'

By midday the whole of the huge works was on strike: 'Either to make sure the news would reach Moscow more quickly, or to prevent troops and tanks from moving in, a large number of women sat down on the tracks to hold up trains, whereupon the men began pulling up the rails and building barriers. Strike action of such boldness is unusual in the history of the Russian workers' movement. Slogans appeared on the works building: "Down with Khrushchev!" and "Use Khrushchev for sausage meat!"'

Meanwhile, police and troops began to move in on the works, which lie four or five kilometres outside Novocherkassk. Thirty ringleaders were arrested in the night. On the morning of 2 June other enterprises, though by no means all of them, came out on strike too. A mass meeting decided on a protest march to demand the release of those arrested. Only 300 strong at first (as Solzhenitsyn says 'you had to be brave') their numbers grew as they approached the town.

When they reached Lenin Square, they found the Party offices full of broken glass — the town authorities had fled to Rostov! 'At the first slight shock the civil authorities hid behind the army.' Small boys climbed on the tanks which trailed the demonstration and tried to block their observation slits. However, there were no students on the march — they'd all been locked in their dormitories since early morning.

Some witnesses say that the captain of the first lot of troops committed suicide rather than open fire on the crowd. According to other sources, his soldiers were all banished to Yakuta for their disobedience. When their replacements fired the first volley, small boys fell down from the trees (they'd climbed up to see better). The dead were carried away in the town buses which for days afterwards went round with bloodstained seats. The demonstrators were filmed. The crowd dispersed, returned and was fired on once more.

'This is what an observant witness saw at 2p.m.: "There are about 8 tanks of different types standing on the square in front of Party headquarters. A cordon of soldiers stands before them. The square is almost deserted, there are only small groups of people, mostly youngsters, standing about and shouting at the soldiers. On the square, puddles of blood have formed in the depressions in the pavement. I am not exaggerating; I never suspected till now that there could be so much blood. The benches in the public gardens are splattered with blood, there are bloodstains on its sanded paths and on the whitewashed tree trunks in the public garden. The whole square is scored with tank tracks. A red flag which the demonstrators had been carrying, is propped against the wall of the Party headquarters, and a gray cap splashed with red-brown blood has been slung over the top of its pole. Across the facade of the Party building hangs a red banner, there for some time past: *The People and the Party are one.*''

Between 5p.m. and 6p.m. the people came back one more ('they were brave those people of Novocherkassk'). By this time six senior members of the Central Committee had flown in. The crowd swelled, and was finally dispersed by tanks and tracer fire by about midnight.

Afterwards, 'the shops were immediately the richer for butter, sausage, and many other things not seen in those parts for a long time, or anywhere outside the capital.'

Most Russians are still completely unaware of what happened — as Solzhenitsyn says: 'Novocherkassk! A whole town rebels — and every trace is licked clean and hidden.' Exactly a week after 'Bloody Saturday' the local radio told the town that the workers at the electric locomotive works had promised to fulfill their plan ahead of schedule.

## Vyshgorod

### ★ Document 2 / June 1969
Appeal of the Residents of the Town of Vyshgorod
to the Central Committee of the Communist Party
of the Union of Soviet Socialist Republics[12]

We, the residents of the town of Vyshgorod in the Kiev-Svyatoshynsk district, are appealing to you for the third time. We ask you to send a commission to Vyshgorod empowered to sort out all the violations of Soviet legality committed by the management of the housing department at the Kremenchuk Hydro-Electric Station and to take the necessary measures to rectify this situation.

On 10 June 1969 the head of the housing department at the Kremenchuk Hydro-Electric Station, comrade Strokov, stated at a meeting that they always lose money on the construction of temporary dwellings, that more is spent on their renovation than we, the inhabitants of these workers' settlements, pay in rent. In reality, not a single nail has been hammered into a single house ever since they were built.

Where are all those thousands of roubles comrade Strokov says have been spent? Ever since the first year of their construction the roofs of almost all the temporary dwellings have leaked, the walls of the barracks are cracking and coming apart, and some of the houses are in an uninhabitable and dangerous condition.

Many of us, on many occasions have approached the deputy manager of the housing department, comrade Abramov, with questions about the repair of our living quarters. All he did was throw people out of his office. Both the management of the housing department and the leadership of the social organisations refused to call a meeting in order to prevent us from voicing our complaints and demanding an improvement in our living conditions. This is why the housing committee of the workers' settlement of Berizka decided to call its own meeting which was attended by inhabitants of all the temporary workers' settlements. The heads of the housing department were also invited.

At this meeting we elected a delegation and sent it to you. The management of the housing department immediately announced that our meeting was illegal. We sent a delegation straight to Moscow because questions about the allocation of additional funds for the repair and construction of housing can be decided upon by no-one but the Council of Ministers. When our representatives set out to see you, unprecedented outrages took place at the construction site. But first the good points must be mentioned.

They started to repair our houses. The streets, which are used as playgrounds by our children, were closed to traffic, and road works were begun. For all this a word of thanks should be given to our management. But they literally cannot sleep when you do not pat them over the head for their labours. They tried to save face and made such a muddle of things that talk of their scandalous behaviour went far beyond Kiev.

For the first time in the history of the existence of workers' settlements, the directors of all government departments, chief engineers and other leading executives visited the settlement of Berizka, where the above mentioned meeting took place, and also other settlements where the workers live in temporary housing. They insisted that we elect a new housing committee, alleging that the one elected by us was not approved by the management ... and therefore illegal. We demanded that they should approve our housing committee, and categorically refused to elect a new one. We understood perfectly why they so urgently needed a new housing committee: they wanted to show you that the comrades we sent to Moscow as our representatives were imposters, that no-one elected and authorised them to ask your help in the name of the builders of the Kiev Hydro-Electric Station.

But we were not taken in by this. Sensible people would have stopped at this and not started to stir up further trouble. But our local management is not of this kind. All the residents refused to co-operate, but they nevertheless managed to gether together 30 people, who were in no way our authorised representatives, in the community hall. They then 'elected': a new housing committee in the presence of Lavrenchuk and his troops.[13] After this, they began to persecute those who had actively supported our housing committee at the above meeting and who had played an active part in the work of the old housing committee.

People were summoned to the police station and intimidated. Then, on 10 June, a meeting of the residents of the workers' settlement was called by the local authorities for the first time in the history of the Kiev Hydro-Electric Station. Leading executives arrived from the city of Kiev for this meeting. We saw the representative of the Kiev-Svyatoshynsk local Party executive committee for the first time. He couldn't even find the time to come and welcome us earlier when the town of Vyshgorod was being born, built by our own hands.

The meeting was stormy: we raised our painful questions about our houses, we explained how and for what reasons they sacked people, how internal passports were not issued to us in violation of our basic rights[14] and how residents who were permanently registered in the Berizka settlement were moved to other districts. We also explained that workers, who travelled to the Treplisk Hydro-Electric Station building site were not paid for a long period of time, so that many of them were forced to give up their jobs on the site. We pointed out how the local administration took advantage of the lack of supervision by higher ranking bodies by allowing all kinds of corruption to creep in in the allocation of housing. We also brought up the fact that we had to travel several kilometres to the military registration and enlistment office, located in Svyatoshyn, that the Party and sports organisations are in the Podilsk district, while social organisations are for some reasons situated in Dymer, and so on. We also mentioned that the bus ran for several days to Berizka and then allegedly 'fell into the lake'. In such a short letter we cannot explain everything.

We were pleased with the meeting. Colonel Lavrenchuk, who introduced himself as the Deputy Head of the Regional Administration of the Ministry of Internal Affairs and as the representative of the regional Party organisation, spoke towards the end of the meeting. He assured us that all these shortcomings would be eliminated, that by 1972 all of us would receive permanent housing, and that no-one was going to be arrested. He also said that the delegation we'd sent to see you would be allowed to speak at a similar meeting in the community centre, on condition that they first asked the local administration and didn't call 'illegal meetings'.

We believed Colonel Lavrenchuk and took him at his word. But oh, how bitterly mistaken we were. On 13 June, the management of the housing department called a meeting of the remaining inhabitants of the temporary settlements. By this time our representatives had come back from seeing you, and the head of our housing committee, comrade I.A.Hrushchuk, relying on Colonel Lavrenchuk's promise, asked for the report of the delegation which travelled to Moscow to be included on the agenda.

The whole situation couldn't have been simpler. They promised and we believed them. All we wanted was the right to speak and then everything would have fallen into place. But this did not happen: at this meeting the management surpassed even themselves. It all began when only very short notice for the meeting was given, and only those who just managed to get into the hall were admitted to the meeting. For all others the doors were closed. A chairman and secretary for the meeting were not elected. The Party organiser, Velychko, appointed himself chairman of the meeting and declared that no delegation had been sent to Moscow by anyone and that today none of us would be allowed to speak. He then added that the speech would be given by comrade Strokov after which only 'essential' questions would be answered, and that the meeting would then come to an end.

Where and when, under what regime, have meetings ever been conducted like this? When comrade Strokov started speaking the people left out on the street hammered on the door while those inside demanded that they be let in. After a considerable struggle the people outside got into the hall, which became completely full. People asked for permission to speak, but Velychko gave no-one the opportunity to do so. To the numerous questions that poured in from all sides, Velychko replied that they were not 'essential'. When in his opinion all 'essential' questions had been dealt with, he closed the meeting. But people would not leave the hall. They demanded the Hryshchuk and the other delegates be allowed to speak. Encouraged by the show of solidarity among all the workers present, they climbed onto the stage but Velychko, the Party organiser, behaved like a disgusting hooligan. He shoved a woman with a child, he forcibly grabbed the microphone from Hryshchuk and then cut the lead. Colonel Lavrenchuk, the 'good Colonel' who had promised to allow the delegation to speak, summoned a detachment of police officers into the hall to arrest our delegates.

Comrades! What is this? Have you ever seen such a thing? One forms the impression that our arrogant and deceitful 'good-for-nothing directors' deliberately provoked us to rebel.

Is it possible that they do not understand the simple truth that our enemies are just waiting for something like this to happen in our country? Why is it that we, simple workers, understand this?

We did not fall for this provocation. We stopped them arresting our delegates, and then calmed down and started to listen to Hryshchuk. Hryshchuk picked up a copy of the Constitution and said, 'Comrades, in the Constitution it is written ... '; and at that very moment music and sirens were turned on in the hall as if to say 'go into the streets and hold your meeting there' — this would have been that 'illegal meeting' whose instigators they had the right to arrest. Isn't that what it amounts to?

But we didn't fall for this. When people gathered around Hryshchuk outside the hall, he said only one thing: 'Let us calmly break up the meeting and go home. The Central Committee of the Communist Party does not know that the management of the housing department has lied to this extent! We shall go to them again and explain everything.'

After Hryshchuk's departure a scurrillous piece about him appeared in the newspaper *Evening Kiev* [24 June] which can only be described as typical of market-place gossip. Next day we learnt that Hryshchuk had been arrested.

Comrades! We do not believe that this arrest took place with your knowledge and we seriously ask you to take the delegation, which brings you this letter, under your protection. As far as our requests are concerned, we will voice them when your representatives come to us. Do not believe those who call us rebels, do not believe them when they tell you that we demand housing immediately, on a silver platter. We want to wait our turn honestly. But we want an assurance that the waiting list is genuine, that every one of us, be it in one, two or five years time, will obtain suitable housing, and that no one will try to obstruct this process. We are not afraid of work, and if necessary, we will roll up our sleeves and build these houses after work, just as we built our settlement, Berizka. Please get us right.

The Kremenchuk Hydro-Electric Station Reservoir is still needed and will be needed for a long time. This means that we, the workers at this Reservoir, will also be needed. We ask one thing: let those who arrested Hryshchuk release him, for he is the same sort of person as we are.

Comrades, we believe in you, the leaders of our country and our Party. We ask you to believe in us and send your representatives to Vyshgorod. As regards the management of the housing department of the Kremenchuk Hydro-Electric Station, they have been so deceitful that we no longer believe one word of what they say, and we will never again work on a building site with them.

In conclusion, we want to say that there will be no incidents in our workers' settlement. We will await your reply patiently. But if our letter does not reach you, we will go on sending our representatives with the same letter until you finally receive it.

# 3:

# The Right to Protest
## Introduction

This is a collection of documents about three individual workers, who dared to raise their voices in protest against the Soviet government. They are the confused, contradictory political searchings of uneducated workers. One is a socialist, one a nationalist and one friendly with a right-wing slavophile. Their views couldn't be more different, but in the eyes of the Soviet government they are the same — *opposition* — and they have all been treated in exactly the same way: their flats have been ransacked, they've been beaten, thrown into prison, labour camps and psychiatric hospitals.

Nikolay Yevgrafov is a Ukrainian worker who had a job as a loader in Slavyansk. Presumably because of the war, he never got farther than the third class in school. His protest is addressed to 'all activists of the Communist and Socialist Parties' in the West. In it he speaks out against the 'Asiatic psuedo-communism of the Soviet state' which 'uses Marxism as a cover'. In 1977 he also signed a samizdat appeal by nine political prisoners, including another of our three, Rebryk, complaining about the beatings administered to political prisoners in the prison camp at Mordovia.

Gennady Bogolyubov, on the other hand, believes that 'there's no difference between Stalinism and fascism'. He got on the KGB's list when he began corresponding with Vladimir Osipov, and reading his journal *Veche* (the name of a medieval assembly). Osipov is a sort of modern-day slavophile (the slavophiles were nostalgic and usually religious admirers of Russia's medieval past, opponents of everything modern and Western). He was sent to Siberia for seven years in 1961 and then was arrested again and sentenced in 1975 to eight years in a strict labour camp. The KGB also found copies of Solzhenitsyn's *The Gulag Archipelago* in Bogolyubov's possession. In another samizdat document (November 1976) he writes: 'during my period of continuous interrogation by the KGB they brought only *one* charge against me: *sympathy with the writings of A.I. Solzhenitsyn*'. His experiences with the KGB include beatings, surveillance, psychiatric hospital, searches, imprisonment on non-existent drugs charges. They also stole his passport. As he says, 'I don't have to remind you what it means in our country to be left without a passport: *I am virtually outside the law and can be arrested at any minute*'.[1] Bogolyubov's political confusion is such that, in spite of his right-wing inclinations, he is first and foremost a worker and writes to a Western trade union leader, Harry Bridges, leader of the American dockers' union.

The third worker, Bohdan Rebryk, addresses himself to another American trade union leader, George Meany, head of the AFL-CIO. His concern is 'the tragedy of the whole of the Ukrainian people'. His 'personal tragedy' was that at the age of 18 he 'voluntarily' joined a group of young workers sent to Siberia, theoretically to learn a trade. In fact, this was part of the Soviet government's plan to Russify the Ukraine by sending Ukrainians away and settling Russians there instead.

Between 1959 and 1970 about 800,000 Ukrainians left (mostly young people from the villages) while one million (mostly Russian) settled in the Ukraine.[2] Most of the Russians settled in the industrial cities of the eastern Ukraine (the area which has always been part of the USSR, as opposed to the western Ukraine which was part of Poland until the second world war). From 1926 to 1970 the Russian population in this area increased from 2.7 million to 8.6 million (i.e. by 200 per cent), while the Ukrainian population increased only from 23 to 28 million (only 20 per cent).[3]

Rebryk was later sent to a labour camp for verbally protesting against this 'new nation' plan. According to another samizdat document Rebryk has been severely beaten on three occasions. After one beating in a prison in Lvov he was thrown into a cell and 'they specially emptied a couple of pails of water onto the cement floor and told me to ask God to dry it!' (Like many nationalists, he is religious.)

Appeal to the Activists
of the Communist and Socialist Parties
Nikolay Andreyevich Yevgrafov, Ukrainian:

*Beginning lost ...*

The ethics of the bureaucrats, which crush the individual and produce in his place a whittled down and deceitful conformist. This is the inevitable fruit of the Soviet regime, the result of the concentration of power in the hands of the party clique or of one man. The aim of Soviet power is to train Soviet people to behave and think mechanically, to organise and stereotype their every thought so that no-one will dare to cast doubt on the sanctity of the status quo. This power bases itself on the silent and terrified majority. It possesses a huge and sensitive machine of spiritual and physical oppression. It stamps out all protest, whether it takes political or other forms.

Given this situation, the authorities are not satisfied with persecuting dissidents and curtailing their activities. However faint the whisper of unorthodoxy, they use spies and searches, to try to read what goes on in people's minds and hearts. They punish suggestions, ideas and intentions with dismissals, arrests, exile and deportation. Soviet society has been transformed into a vast police-school. Its people (that is, a significant proportion of them) are being turned into dummies whose very thoughts wear uniforms, moral and mental eunuchs, servants of the Soviet government and state. Only at the cost of enormous efforts have a few Soviet people succeeded in preserving their individuality, their living souls. And this small handful of isolated individuals scattered across the country has dared to challenge the Soviet bureaucratic system and is struggling against it. Amidst the universal cowardice and demoralisation these people have stepped forward to champion human rights.

In spite of the repressive measures used by the Soviet tyranny, the pulse of social consciousness is beginning to beat more strongly in our country. One can feel that the Russian intelligentsia is beginning to wake up, and with it the intelligentsia of the nations enslaved by Russia. Feelings of citizenship, national consciousness, and dignity, lukewarm until now, are beginning to revive. Educated people are beginning to protest in samizdat and the foreign press, though the simple people as yet remain silent. These few

89

individuals understand that life without human rights — is no life. They are beginning to understand that a man deprived of his freedom is a man no longer. They are unmasking the deeds of Soviet tyranny. They are defending freedom and human rights. The Soviet government fears nothing so much as exposure and is crushing them with all the means at its disposal.

Therefore I turn to you, to all true communists and socialists, to all who represent the workers. I ask you to speak out against the Asiatic pseudo-communism of the Soviet state, and raise your voices in protest and in defence of human rights in the USSR. Soviet totalitarianism is using Marxism as a cover. It must be put in the stocks. The Soviet government must hear the voice of the progressive forces of the world, the cry of honourable people, of all those for whom the way forward lies in social justice, peace and freedom, and liberate the innocent people who are suffering for their convictions. You as the representatives of human conscience and social justice must speak out loud and clear and force the hypocritical and despotic Soviet government to listen to you. I hope that Soviet dissidents will find support and solidarity among the activists of the *Communist and Socialist Parties*.


Appendix:
An Extract from My Verdict
'On 29 April 1975 the Judicial Collegium for Criminal Cases of the Donetsk Regional Court examined in closed session the charges against N.A.Yevgrafov, born in 1930, Ukrainian, citizen of the USSR, educated to the third grade, a bachelor, earlier sentenced under article 62 section 1 of the Criminal Code of the Ukrainian SSR to seven years' imprisonment, released from prison in 1973, works as a loader in Slavyansk.[4]

'The Judicial Collegium has established that after his release from the place where he had been imprisoned for anti-Soviet agitation and propaganda he did not take the road of repentance, and continued to indulge in subversive activities against Soviet society and the Soviet authorities. For example, the accused used abstracts from the work of foreign sociologists, philosophers and economists, brought from his place of imprisonment, which contained anti-Soviet remarks. He wrote an anti-Soviet libel which he called 'truth about untruth' and gave it to his friends to read. In addition, the accused spread ideas of an anti-Soviet character among the workers. In the court-sitting the accused did not admit his guilt, and explained to the court that he had committed the above-mentioned deeds, but without any aim of subverting or undermining Soviet society or the state. In choosing an appropriate punishment for Yevgrafov, the court, taking into consideration the socially dangerous nature of the crime, the character of the accused, the fact that he was earlier sentenced for a similar crime, brings in the verdict that he is an especially dangerous and hardened criminal. Yevgrafov is ordered to pay legal costs of 232 roubles. The court sentences him to ten years' imprisonment in a corrective labour camp (ITK), under special regime.'

★ Document 2
Open Letter
to Harry Bridges from
Gennady Aleksandrovich Bogolyubov,
a worker with twenty years' trade union experience
a Soviet citizen,
on the subject of your conversation with
the TASS correspondent in Washington
on 12 April 1977

I, a worker in the painting and plastering trade, am writing to you in reply to what you said on the subject of 'human rights' in our country.

I would never have written to you, if you, Mr Harry Bridges, hadn't given an interview to the TASS [official Soviet news agency] correspondent, which moved me to the depths of my soul.[5] I will remind you: 'As a worker' you say 'I notice in particular that there is not one representative of the working class among the Soviet "dissidents" and traitors to their country'.

You were greatly mistaken, Mr Harry Bridges, yes, whoever told you this. Particularly if you take into account the fact that a people of 250 million is living without any elementary information, and news of the life of this people only 'trickles through' to you.

There are many 'dissidents' among the workers in our country who are fighting for their human rights, but they are viciously crushed by blackmail, by provocation and above all by the organs of the KGB. These people are tried in court for crimes they didn't

91

commit. They, so to speak, fabricate a 'case' against them, put them in a camp, and if the man doesn't turn over a new leaf, then they fabricate another charge. Take, for example, my friend Viktor Kuz'mich Gridasov, a worker, born in 1943. In 1972 in Magadansk region, he was summoned to court as a witness and right there in court was charged under article 206, ch.1.[6] He received one year's imprisonment. On 26 November 1976 he was arrested at my flat supposedly for violation of the passport law under article 197 UK RSFSR[7] and was sentenced to six months' imprisonment under strict regime, although there are thousands of people who aren't registered living here in Magadansk. Before he'd been freed from the camp they stuck another charge on him under article 190-1 UK RSFSR.[8] He was accused of being a traitor and of slandering the Soviet system. It's difficult for the ordinary American in your free country to understand how they trample a person's rights in our country if he struggles for the implementation of the basic points of the Constitution of the USSR.

My friend at work, Ivan Vasil'yevich Bely, has worked for 20 years in the building trade in Magadansk as a plasterer in UOR (the Department of Decorating) in the 'Magadansk Town Building Trust'. He has been trying for many years to get a flat, since he lives in a nine metre room with his family of four people. He naively waited, thinking that his turn ought to come and he would get his long awaited flat. But it turned out that his application to the trade union committee had been lost. Then he began to complain. The head of the Department said 'Why don't you complain to the UN?'. Bely wrote to the UN. Only his letter didn't arrive. Next he had a talk with the authorities and sometime later, on his way home from work, worker Ivan Vasil'yevich Bely, was brutally beaten by unknown men.

And now it's time to speak about me. I was born in 1942 into a family of hereditary weavers. My ancestors even worked as weavers in the factory of Savva Morozov.[9] After the end of the seven-year plan I went to work as an apprentice plasterer. I worked in the building trade until I was called up. In 1962 I went to serve in the Soviet army; in 1964 I was injured and became an invalid of the third class of the Soviet army. In spite of my health, I worked for many years at physically heavy work. Then I went to the far east. There, in Kolyma, I was treated very unjustly, and I began to write complaints in all directions and all to no avail. Only, the organs of the KGB began to persecute me dreadfully, eavesdropping on my telephone conversations, intercepting my letters, etc. They searched my flat three times without a Procurator's warrant. The authorities have rich imaginations. The first search was carried out on the pretext that I was keeping firearms in my flat; the second that I was keeping explosives; the third — I was hiding a criminal; the fourth, on 9 October 1976, on the pretext that I was keeping drugs there. I was blamed for having sleeping pills 'Noksiron' which I'd received by legal means. I hadn't taken one tablet myself, but I gave the drug to Zinov'yev, who under pressure testified against me at the inquiry.

This, Mr Bridges, is what it's still like here. True, there's a popular saying: you can give a dog a bad name and hang him for it. And look, he's a criminal already. And also, as you, unthinkingly, cry — a criminal, a fascist and a traitor.

Do you know that when I, an invalid of the Soviet army, came from Magadansk to Moscow for treatment, I was put in a hospital for invalids on 14 January and chucked out on the 24th on the demand of the authorities? After this monstrous and barbaric treatment of a sick man and an invalid of the armed forces, am I to become a model citizen? Never. I was charged on the same day under article 224, section 2 of the Criminal Code of the RSFSR (from 6 to 15 years).[10]

After being thrown out of hospital in Moscow I was knocked down at Riga station by a 'Volga' car, as a result of which I ended up in the neurosurgical department NII of the Sklifosovsky casualty unit and was diagnosed as having serious multiple head and brain injuries and a fractured right-temporal bone. But I've got two children, my daughter Katya aged five and my son Sergey aged nine. In the east I earned 500 roubles a month, now 120. One can't live on this amount of money.

I remember a conversation I had with a captain of the KGB in Magadansk. In a fit of rage I told him that, as a worker, I'd turn to the leaders of the Communist movement — Georges Machais and Enrico Berlinguer. To this the KGB man Povolaretsky replied that the time would come when they too would be put in Kolyma. I wasn't surprised and replied that 'Stalin, who is obviously your ideological mentor, put the whole of the Third International in jail and left millions of Russians to rot in the concentration camps of Noril'sk, Magadan, Vorkuta and other places. And if you get your way, you'll put the whole world behind barbed wire'. This conversation took place on 9 December 1976. And in the same year the KGB gave the signal for me to be thrown out of the health resort 'Thaw' in Magadansk region, supposedly for breaking the rules. And on 9 October my flat was searched and criminal charges were brought against me.

In conclusion, I can tell you, Harry Bridges, that I changed my convictions after reading the works of Alexander Isayevich Solzhenitsyn, for which I was persecuted by the KGB. I'll say one thing — *The Gulag Archipelago* carries on.

We condemn the lawlessness in China and the violation of human rights there. I'll say one thing — there's a good Russian proverb: 'If your cow moos, don't tell other people's cows to shut up'. This proverb relates to you, Mr Harry Bridges. You can give what interviews you like — it doesn't matter to you. But for this open letter I may be locked up for a spell or thrown into psychiatric care. And if the public doesn't stick up for me, then I'll lie in a looney bin for years.

I know that in your country there are cases of violation of human rights. But sentences are passed in open court in front of the public, in order to avoid the multiplication of such cases. But here, in the whole history of Soviet power not one line has been written to say that dissidents are imprisoned in madhouses.

You write that 'Soviet dissidents are paid agents of the CIA'. And you're whose agent — the KGB's? You are to all intents and purposes defending Stalin's regime. This means that you're fostering fascism since for me there's no difference between Stalinism and fascism.

To conclude my letter I would like to give you some advice: before talking about Soviet dissidents, put yourself in our place and try to approach this question seriously and scientifically.

Yours sincerely,

Citizen of the USSR,
*G.A. Bogolyubov*

★ **Document 3 / December 1976**

Letter to George Meany

*In a letter addressed to George Meany, leader of the AFL-CIO,*
*38-year-old Ukrainian political prisoner Bohdan Rebryk, who is*
*incarcerated in Mordovian prison camp Uch. Zh. Kh. 385/1, writes:*

I am appealing to you as leader, and through you, to the workers united in the biggest trade union in America.[11] I am a Ukrainian worker who has become a victim of the permanent arbitrary rule in the USSR, and under the conditions of the Soviet totalitarian regime I am deprived of any rights of defence. The point here is not my own personal tragedy but the tragedy of the whole of the Ukrainian people. A short account of my life will show what rights and freedoms a worker enjoys in my country.

Today the Soviet government attempts to demonstrate to the whole world that people such as I do not exist — only now and then, 'renegade', 'brigand', 'dissident'!!!, appear in the Soviet apologetic press. But judge for yourselves. I was born in 1938 in Ivano-Frankovsk in the Ukraine. My mother was killed by fascists in 1942 for saving the lives of a Jewish family. In 1949 my father was arrested by the NKVD as a result of a false denunciation, and as an 'enemy of the people' he was sent to the concentration camps in Kolyma. My father was rehabilitated in 1956 and died in 1957. After having finished elementary school in my native town, I went to study in Magnitogorsk, in Russia, at the FZO[12] school there. I worked a carpenter on construction sites in Magnitorgorsk. The monthly wage was 60-70 roubles. I was looked upon as a good worker.

In October 1957 I was called up into the army where I was trained as an aerial-gunner radio operator … In 1962 I lost 70 per cent of my vision in the execution of my duties. I was discharged from the army and returned home to the Ukraine.

Already during the first days in my native country I was struck by the fact that in all Ukrainian institutions and enterprises the Russian language was predominant. At first I accepted what I had been taught by teachers at school and political instructors in the army, that is that the Russian language is multi-national. But I quickly realised the matter was more complicated. Everywhere the language of my people is treated as an inferior language, it is denigrated, and those who use it are hounded and persecuted. And all this is done by newly-arrived Russians, whom, by order of the regime, I should respectfully address as 'elder brothers', and 'liberators'. More than that, my native language has become my enemy. Use of it has led to me being identified as a Ukrainian bourgeois nationalist. But this is not only a moral and national debasement, it also means that I can only get a hard, badly-paid job. The result is that a large part of the able-bodied Ukrainian population is forced to seek work in Siberia, Kazakhstan, or beyond the polar region; they are forced to leave the Ukraine — 'voluntarily' at that.

The enforced russification with which I came into contact contradicted the principles and ideals of my life; even more, according to my then naive convictions, they contradicted the Constitution of the USSR. Feeling myself to be a son of the Ukrainian people, I could not reconcile myself to the thought that my nation stands on the verge of genocide. I made a stand in defence of the honour and dignity of my people. This sacred obligation of every citizen cost me three years imprisonment.[13] After being released from the prison camp, I was placed in a situation in which I once again discovered that my people, who number 50 million, do not have the right to defend their own culture. Only after 10 months of extreme poverty did I, with difficulty, obtain a job as a loader in a furniture factory. But in May 1974 I was again arrested. I quote a few words from my verdict, from the official document. Here we are only concerned with the most imortant charges against me:

1. 'Had in his possession, in his apartment, handwritten texts of the 17th-18th century agreements, between Ukraine and the Muscovite state, on the annexation of Ukraine to Russia'.[14] The KGB pronounced the texts of both documents to be 'anti-Soviet'.

2. 'Made a recording of a national song on his own tape-recorder.' This refers to a Ukrainian folksong from the times of Khmelnytsky.[15]

3. 'Made a present, to a friend, of a book with a national theme, with his own dedication.' In reality this was an excerpt from a poem by O.Oles, legally published in Kiev in 1970.[16]

4. 'Expressed the opinion that the Ukraine is being russified.'

5. 'Listened to the bourgeois radio stations *Voice of America* and *Radio Liberty*.'

Of course, according to the verdict I did all this with the aim of 'undermining the Soviet state': 'The people's court attentively scrutinised the crime', and declared that I was a criminal separatist. The sentence — seven years strict regime and three years exile in Siberia.

Soviet propaganda proclaims to the whole world that each republic within the USSR is an independent and sovereign country. In fact, each Soviet republic is a colony of Russia …

*Mr President!* By this appeal I want to bring to the attention of every worker of your big country the inhuman conditions in which the workers of my country have to live and work, and the 'rights' which they enjoy. Once again I want to stress, that my own personal tragedy is not an isolated instance, but a mass phenomenon in the USSR. It is a tragedy for everyone, and in the first place for my Ukrainian people … I can confirm this under oath as a Christian, and if need be with my life.

Yours very sincerely

*Bohdan Rebryk*
December 1976

# 4:

# The Right to Emigrate
## Introduction

Many states make immigration difficult. The USSR is one of them. A few states make emigration difficult. Again the USSR is one of them. It's not quite so bad if you're a Jew, a German, or a world famous dissident, with people behind you (100,000 Jews left in 1971-74), but if you're a worker ...

These documents present the cases of four would-be emigrés. As the Helsinki group says: 'These people live in different places, but one thing unites them — they are all workers, representatives of what, according to official Soviet ideology, is the "ruling" class in the USSR.'[1] Like the Klebanov group their initial criticisms of the regime are mostly economic. It is only when they are persecuted for complaining about their working and living conditions that they add civil rights to their demands.

This is particularly true in the case of Leonid Sery, who has been trying to get out at least since 1975. He has seven small children[2] whom he claims are starving to death. After he 'was persecuted for [his] demands for a better standard of living and pay' he developed a political programme, which includes: independent trade unions; real elections to all positions of political power; and rights for the nationalities. (This is one of the few documents in which the national question comes up.)

In the last few years Sery has written an absolutely enormous number of petitions. Inside the Soviet Union he has appealed to Brezhnev, the 25th Congress of the CPSU (16 February 1976), and we have no idea how many state organs. Abroad, he has written to George Meany, President of the American trade union federation, AFL-CIO (10 June 1976 and February 1978); the governments of the USA, England, Canada, Australia, the Federal Republic of Germany, and France; the International Committee for Human Rights; the International Red Cross (September 1976); Jimmy

Carter (autumn 1977); Ukrainians in the USA (autumn 1977) and in Canada (November 1977); the ILO, and the International Committee of Free Trade Unions (27 March 1978).

Though we have no evidence that Sery is in any way connected with the Free Trade Union Association, he comes out strongly in its defence. In a letter of February 1978 he writes: 'I beg you Mr Meany, to defend Klebanov and his group, to obtain their release from prison and also to give the newly created free trade union in the USSR all possible moral and financial aid.' On 16 April the Odessa KGB called him in and warned him 'not to keep in contact with the West, and that the Free Trade Union will not be allowed to develop, but will be strangled at birth.' The KGB major added that Sery is officially warned to end his activity in defence of rights. Sery's wife, Valentina, informs us that he may be arrested.[3]

Another of these workers, Valentin Ivanov, finally got an exit visa on 28 August 1977 — 18 years after he put in his first application! In 1959 he tried to escape across the border into Turkey (as far as we know about 200 of these attempts take place each year on the Turkish and Finnish borders of the Soviet Union). He was caught and sentenced to three years in a labour camp. In the autumn of 1966 he applied to emigrate and was forcibly interned in a psychiatric hospital. In 1976 he tried again, and when he didn't get an answer staged a one-man demonstration with a placard in the centre of Moscow (21 September 1976). He was arrested within ten minutes and conveyed back to his home town of Kuibyshev in Siberia.

Ivanov later related his workmates' response to his one-man demonstration: 'Valya, it won't do you any good, don't you understand? So you protested — you were arrested. If the whole of our brigade protested — we'd just be beaten up by the druzhenniki. [4] If the whole town protested — they'd simply cut us down with machine-gun fire as they did at Novocherkassk in 1962.'[5]

On 14 June 1977 Ivanov determinedly staged his second one-man demonstration. Again he was arrested but this time he was taken to the infamous Psychiatric Hospital No.7 in Moscow, where many of the members of the Free Trade Union Association were also held. He was released after seven days. The KGB were so anxious to get rid of him that they told him that he would be allowed to emigrate without even paying the usual 800 roubles for his visa. He's now in the USA. Persistence can sometimes pay off even in the USSR!

These four workers took their stories to Yuri Orlov who, for publishing documents like these, was sentenced on 18 May 1978 to 12 years (seven in a labour camp, and five in internal exile). The papers prepared by his defence counsel in London, John Mac-Donald QC, (who was not allowed to appear at his trial), contain a statement signed by Lyudmilla Alekseyeva (a member of the Helsinki monitoring group), explaining how the statements of these workers saw the light of day:

re: *Emigration Document* 13 [Document 1 below]

'*1. Document 13 which the Group issued gives particulars of four working families who wished to emigrate from the USSR.*

'*2. The Group received a letter from a worker in Odessa, Leonid Sery. Both Orlov and I knew his wife and talked to her. She had a photograph of her six children with her. They had no shoes. I collected old clothes and what I could find to send her for her children. In his letter Leonid Sery says that they had only about 20 roubles a month per head to feed their family. From my own experience I know that it would be very difficult to feed someone for as little as that.*

'*3. Valentin Ivanov came to Moscow and brought all his documents with him. He lives alone and Orlov was worried about him, so he asked me to keep in touch with him. For several months I spoke to him once a week on the telephone. I continued to do this until I left Moscow in February 1977.*

'*4. I remember that several members of the Group and Amalrik used to talk about Ivan Sivak, but I did not meet him.*

'*5. I did, however, meet Vladimir Pavlov. He came to Moscow to find the Group. He did not know anyone in Moscow and so he stopped people in the street and asked them if they could direct him to the flat of Orlov or Sakharov. He stopped many people. Finally someone said they would take him there. They drove round Moscow in a taxi until they reached the house of a painter named Sasha. Sasha gave them Orlov's address. We were very surprised about this because no member of the group knew a painter called Sasha. This is a very good example of the way people sought us out.*

'*6. Pavlov brought his documents with him. We questioned him carefully and I am satisfied his story is true.*'

100

## ★ Document 1 / 2 December 1976
## Four Workers Who Want to Emigrate
## for Economic and Political Reasons[6]

*Valentin Anatolevich Ivanov*: Russian; born in 1930; electrician; place of residence — Settlement of Yermolino, Kaluzhsk Region, RSFSR. On 3 August 1976, in his petition to the Presidium of the Supreme Soviet of the USSR, he wrote:

'On the basis of the law of citizenship of the USSR, and also article 14 of the Universal Declaration of Human Rights, and the Final Act of the Helsinki Conference, I ask for permission to leave the USSR.

'I am a Russian worker aged 46. I have worked in production for 30 years, 22 of these on electrical repairs. In the archives of the KGB there are three folders of documents which confirm that I am a skilled electrician, conscientious in my work, practically don't drink and don't smoke.

'I will list some of the reasons which led me in 1959 to take the risk of illegally crossing the border, in 1964 and 1966 to ask for permission to emigrate and now to apply to the Presidium again with this request.

'1. The low level of pay. I can say on my own responsibility, that I have spent the best years of my life slaving for a crust of bread.

'2. The lack of free trade unions leaves the worker totally at the mercy of the arbitrary will of the administration. For example, in September 1974 I was forced to work for twenty hours over Saturday and Sunday and was paid nothing for it.[7] The trade union, which I turned to with a complaint, took the side of the administration. One could give dozens of such examples.

'3. The absence of an independent and objective court. This was the only reason judge Aliyev in Baku convicted me in autumn 1976, supposedly for trying to cross the border illegally. The case was rigged by the Azerbaidzhan KGB, and Aliyev cooperated with

101

them to the utmost, with no regard for professional norms.

'4. The cruel and humiliating treatment men receive in the labour camps. I can speak of this from experience, since I have spent many days in freezing solitary confinement in Camp No.8 of the Omsk UMZ.[8] There I not only endured the usual physical effects of hunger and cold, but was also given nothing to drink for 36 hours on the orders of Major Polyakov.

'5. The continual and ever growing tendency of the KGB to use psychiatry to strengthen its inquisitorial and punitive powers. Thus, in autumn 1966 Captain Talanov, an investigator for the Azerbaidzhan KGB, sent me to the psychiatric hospital because I would not confess my guilt. At least, that is what he told me before I sent sent off. When I returned from the hospital 20 days later and again refused to confess, Talanov began to threaten to transfer me back to the hospital again.

'In autumn 1972 in Omsk Lieutenant Colonel Udovydchenko gave orders to transfer me to the psychiatric hospital, and the chief doctor of this hospital, who had never set eyes on me, automatically commanded me to be transferred to the department where the raving lunatics are kept. Fortunately, the doctor on duty that evening suspected something, and on her own authority countermanded that murderous order. Seven days later I was pronounced healthy ...

'Experience has shown that the authorities ignore this sort of petition, therefore I am addressing a copy of it to the US embassy asking them to publish it in the free press. In this way I hope to bring it to the notice of our government, to attract the attention of Western society, and above all of the Western workers, to the situation of the Russian worker who tries to defend his economic interests and his human dignity.'

On 21 December 1976 V.A.Ivanov appeared in the Square of the Revolution in Moscow with a placard: 'To the Soviet authorities. I demand permission to emigrate. I have gone through hell in your camps and "gas chambers".* What else is left? Russian worker Ivanov V.A.' Ten minutes later Ivanov was seized by the police and spent 24 hours in a police station, after which he was sent home. On 9 November Valentin Ivanov addressed a letter to the

*"dushegubki" — a word used on connection with the Nazis; now perhaps slang for psychiatric hospitals.

President of the AFL-CIO[9] in which he wrote:

'Dear Mr Meany,

'I am a Russian worker, a highly qualified electrician with a thirty year record. I am turning to you as the leader of the American trade unions.

'Since 1949 I have undergone persecution by the KGB here in my native land. First because I refused to read a lecture on Stalin, and later because I tried to uphold the rights of a working man in Russia.

'I have applied to the Soviet authorities several times with a request to emigrate, and each time the answer has been persecution. Now my position has become critical and I have decided to turn to you to request your help in obtaining an invitation from the American electricians' union. I ask you to help me leave Russia and thereby escape new persecution ...'

*Ivan Mikhailovich Sivak*: Ukrainian; born 1926; lives with a wife and three sons in the village of Dubrava in the Dolinsky District of the Ivano-Frankovsk Region.

Soon after the birth of I.M.Sivak his father went to Canada where he lived till his death in 1965. In 1970 I.M.Sivak requested permission to emigrate to Canada. He was refused, since he had no invitation, and they suggested that he apply for emigration to Israel. He agreed, but didn't get permission. Instead, some time later, he was sent to the Ivano-Frankovsk psychiatric hospital. In a letter addressed to L.I.Brezhnev, Ivan Sivak writes:

'I have already lived thirty years in the Soviet Union; I don't live, I simply exist. In these thirty years little has changed in the life of the worker. I live in poverty and need. My pay is barely enough for food. Besides which, everywhere in the Soviet Union there is no justice, no freedom. In all spheres of life there are restrictions. Here, there, and everywhere man feels himself a slave ...

'More than a year has passed since in the capital of Finland, Helsinki, the final act of the Conference on Security and Co-operation in Europe was solemnly signed by leaders of the European countries and the USA, and personally by you. One can say without exaggeration that the government of the Soviet Union not only is not observing the conditions laid down in this document, but is ignoring them, does not take into consideration the opinion of its citizens. I want to remind you that the Declaration of Human Rights is also signed by the government of the Soviet Union. But in

103

fact in the Soviet Union man is deprived of being the master of his fate ...

'I once more ask you personally, Leonid Il'ich, give me permission to emigrate with my family to Israel.'

In a letter addressed to the Helsinki monitoring group, I.M.Sivak asks for 'help in emigrating to Israel or to any country of the free world'.

*Vladimir Maksimovich Pavlov*: Russian; born 1929; a bus driver. He lives with a wife and son in the town of Maikop. His conflicts with the authorities date back to 1949 when he was condemned to two years imprisonment for hooliganism. According to the Helsinki monitoring group this is what happened:

'In 1949 as a young man he worked as a driver in the Urals. In front of their hostel stood a statue of Stalin with one arm held out. One night someone hung an old battered shoe from Stalin's outstretched arm. The organs of state security thought it essential to react to this in some way. They arrested Pavlov, whom they already knew to be capable of unorthodox behaviour. During the six months which V.M.Pavlov spent in prison waiting for his trial, no evidence whatsoever was discovered against him. Obviously by that time the affair of the shoe already belonged to the past and it was decided not to make a political case out of it. The investigator said to Pavlov: "You understand, that we can't simply let you go. Do you expect us to apologise to you? Here we have a statement that you started a fight in the hostel. Choose: either you confess to this and get three years for hooliganism, or we will make it a political case." The fight in the hostel really had taken place, although Pavlov was in no way its instigator, but had simply defended himself. However in this situation he considered it a blessing 'to confess' in order to escape a much more serious punishment.

'He first petitioned about his wish to emigrate from the USSR in 1966. In 1971 he was condemned to three years' imprisonment under article 190-1 of the Criminal Code of the RSFSR.'[10]

The Helsinki group considers that: 'the verdict in the Pavlov case is one of those documents which reflect the character of the epoch with the utmost clarity and vividness', a typical example of how article 190-1 is used:

Case No. 2-37 / 3 September 1971
Verdict
in the Name of the Russian Soviet Federated
Socialist Republic

The Collegium of the Regional Court of the Adygeisk Autonomous Region ...

Having verified the materials of the preliminary investigation, the Collegium:

Finds

'the accused Pavlov has over a number of years systematically spread, both in an oral and in a written form, deliberate slanders of the Soviet government and state system.

'The crime was committed by him in the town of Maikop during the period 1968-71 under the following circumstances.

'While working as a driver in the Maikop passenger transport services, Pavlov wittingly spread slanders in the neighbourhood. Both by his comments on international events and by exploiting various local troubles, he tried to compromise the policies carried out by the party and government and to discredit the existing state system.

'In spite of conversations of an educative character, repeatedly conducted with him by the administration and the heads of the social organisations of the enterprise, and also official warnings and the employment of the preventive organs of state security on his behalf, the accused Pavlov did not alter his behaviour.

'In 1968 at the time of the events of Czechoslovakia the accused in conversation with the witness Sotnikov uttered slanderous remarks on the subject of the intervention of the combined forces of the socialist states in that country with the aim of preventing a possible restoration of capitalism.

'Later in conversation with the same witness he repeatedly touched on some so-called shortcomings, and made the slanderous declaration that the Communist Party was incapable of eliminating these shortcomings.

'He repeatedly tried to compromise measures carried out to stimulate front-rank workers, systematically slighted them, and expressed satisfaction at the idea of some sort of deeds or crimes being committed against members of the CPSU.

'In 1970 the accused Pavlov spoke approvingly of the hijacking by bandits of an aeroplane in Turkey, only expressing his regret at the fact that he wasn't one of the people who had committed this crime.[11]

'In the course of 1970 in conversation with his colleagues he repeatedly uttered slanders against members of the Communist Party, whom he considers as his ideological enemies. The accused permitted himself similar expressions in reference to witness Chernov, in connection with his election to the party bureau, and in reference to members of the local trade union committee.

'He informed the same witness that, in his view, they had treated the Communist Angela Davis too humanely in the United States of America.[12]

'In 1970-71, the accused Pavlov kept notes for a diary, designed for correspondence with his teenage children, in which he set down his slanders against the Soviet government, and state system. He later gave these notes to Skalyakh, the director of the transport services, to read.

'In May 1971 the accused Pavlov gave the witness Khunganov the weekly *Za Rubezhom*[13] with jottings made by him, aimed at discrediting Soviet democracy.

'In June 1971 the accused Pavlov gave the Regional Trade Union a written statement in which he indicated that he considers the court at his place of work to be incompetent to judge him, Pavlov, in so far as the court was headed by a communist, and also because of 'political considerations. ...

'The Collegium finds that the guilt of the accused Pavlov in the crime committed is correctly defined under article 190-1 of the Criminal Code of the RSFSR and that this is proven by the materials of the case, and confirmed by the oral evidence, verified in the course of the court proceedings.

'Thus the witness Sotnikov corroborated in court that the accused Pavlov uttered slanders on the subject of the events in Czechoslovakia, accusing the countries of the socialist bloc of infringing her liberty and permitted himself a malicious comparison of the actions of the counter-revolutionary, anti-socialist forces there with the progresssive movements in our country in the years of the revolution...

'The witness Khunganov testified that in May 1971 or thereabouts Pavlov slandered Soviet democracy to him and gave him the weekly *Za Rubezhom* with jottings of a similar nature. In addition, according to the testimony of witness Khunganov, the accused in conversation with him approved the behaviour of the German occupiers and expressed his satisfaction that the driver Afanas'yev who crashed, turned out to be a communist.[14]

'Witness Butyrin and Chernov testified to the above-mentioned remarks of the accused about the hijacking of the Soviet aeroplane in Turkey, and witness Chernov in addition to the accused's hostile remarks about the communist Angela Davis.

'Finally, the charges were also confirmed by the material evidence adduced in the case — in the notes for a diary containing Pavlov's misrepresentations, discrediting the government and state system, in his address to the regional trade union, in the jottings on the number of the weekly *Za Rubezhom* adduced in the case.

'The systematic spreading of such slanders, in spite of repeated warnings of their inadmissibility, leads the Collegium to the conclusion that the accused's actions were deliberate.

'In conclusion, taking into consideration the nature of the crime, and the character of the offender, guided by article 301-303 of the Criminal Code of the RSFSR, the Collegium:

Finds

Pavlov Vladimir Maksimovich, guilty under article 190-1 of the Criminal Code of the RSFSR and determines his punishment as three years imprisonment to be served in strict detention in the corrective labour colony, his custody to commence from 20 July 1971.

'The preventative measures against Pavlov, V.M. to be as formerly — detention in custody.

'The material evidence — the exercise books containing notes for a diary — are to be kept in the case.

'The sentence may be appealed against in the period of seven days from the day of its promulgation, and reviewed in the same period from the day of receiving a copy of the sentence in the Supreme Court of the RSFSR.'

Presiding — Kuptsov

People's Assessors — Bogdanova and Gurtenko


Pavlov appealed to the Supreme Court of the RSFSR and received the following reply:

'The validity of the verdict passed on you by the court of the Adygeisk Autonomous Region, is confirmed by the materials of the case, including your testimony during the examination of the case in court. The legal definition of the nature of the crime committed by you, is given by the court correctly, under article 190-1 of the Criminal Code of the RSFSR.

'Due to the absence of grounds for bringing a plea for the revision of the verdict, your request for the re-examination of the case is not complied with.'

p.p. President of the Supreme Court RSFSR

*A.K.Orlov*

10 May 1976

*Leonid Mikhailovich Sery*: 'I work as a lathe operator in the ship-repairing yard of the Il'ichevsky fishing port...My wife doesn't work because our children are young...After all the necessary purchases and payments, we are left with 15-20 roubles a head for food per month. We are always hungry, and because of this the weak fall ill. We are always hungry, especially in the second half of the month ... The doctors tell us that we are physically weak and exhausted. As a result we catch cold. We don't get enough vitamins or fats and this causes low haemoglobin and fainting fits. The children have rickets. All this is the result of a poor diet. But if we ate well, they tell us, we would all be healthy. In spite of the burdens and the deprivation we have to bear, I still try to work better. I hope to persuade my bosses to let me earn enough to feed my large family. I fulfill the norm by 140-150 per cent — one isn't supposed to do more than 140 per cent. I don't drink, don't smoke, don't miss work ...

'The meaning of this exasperating, humiliating, useless correspondence, can only be understood by someone living in the Soviet Union. Here they publicly pretend to give attention to workers' letters, but in fact workers are consulted about nothing. And if they get a particularly awkward customer, then they say to him "Your thoughts are diseased, but we can cure them for you." That's what they said to me in Moscow, in the Central Committee of the CPSU. And in Kiev, when my wife brought a complaint to the Central Committee building, they shipped out a special car to take her away. But thanks to the intervention of a group of outsiders, plasterers who were repairing a building opposite, she got away. Meanwhile, our children fled in all directions ... Seeing all this and experiencing it ourselves, convinces us that in our country the working man does not have the right to protest. The trade unions don't have the right either, but they aren't bothered about it. The only answer we get to our letters is bullying and mockery ...

'Help us, don't let us die from gradual starvation. Shame on our leaders for leaving a worker in a situation where he can't feed his famly. Shame on them for feeding the people with nothing but promises and slogans. Please help us to leave. We'd like to go to America or Canada. In Canada there are Ukrainians too and we'd have less problems with the language. We are Ukrainians too! We will wait as long as we can hold out! We will hope!'[15]

★ **Document 2 / 14 November 1976**
Copy: to the General Secretary of the Central Committee of the CPSU, Leonid Ilich Brezhnev
Open Letter
from citizen Leonid Mikhailovich Sery, a worker,
father of six children ...

We ask you to help us to emigrate from the Soviet Union as soon as we possibly can. We want to go to any of these countries: Canada, the USA, or Australia.

On 16 February 1976 we sent a letter to the 25th Congress of the CPSU. In it we described in great detail the way we live and declared our unwillingness to go on like that. We explained that one can't survive on the minimum wage — 50 roubles a head per month. But we don't even get that.

There are eight of us — myself, my wife and our six children. Our combined income is 195 roubles, plus a 36 rouble allowance for our three children under eight, and 13 roubles from the social security for the baby. There are deductions for taxes, trade union dues, and rent. This leaves about 180-90 roubles.

In general, I want to avoid repetition. In my time I've written lots of letters — to the trade unions, to the newspapers, to the Supreme Soviet and to the Central Committee of the CPSU but YOU wouldn't help or even bother to reply.

All the same, I'll raise certain questions once more. I, not a Party member, but a citizen, a worker, and a trade union member since 1952, officially announce my disagreement with the policies of the Party and the Government on the following questions:

1a. Wage increases are very small and restricted. In our pay office they tell us — we won't let you get more than 140 per cent of the norm.

b. The rates and norms are often revised. However hard you work, you can barely make five or six roubles a day, i.e. hardly anything more than the average. There's no improvement in working conditions. Techniques don't change and we're always short of equipment. I have to bring my own tools to work. What's happening is that they're squeezing more blood and sweat out of the worker. And they're paying him less.

2a. Since 1961 prices have risen sharply in our country. In the state shops there has been an increase of 30-40 per cent in such basic foodstuffs as bread, eggs, butter and other high-energy products. In the collective farm market the price of honey, lard, oil, cream, fruit and vegetables has also risen 1½-2 times.

b. The amount that can be bought in shops is rationed in the following way: 2 kilos of bread; 1 kilo of flour and pasta; 1 kilo of sugar; half a kilo of fat, butter and other products.

c. Meat, butter, potatoes, carrots, cabbage and all sorts of other things are often unavailable.

d. They have closed down lots of grocery stores and opened 'Vodka-Wine' shops on every corner. Our children are being brought up on vodka.

3a. What about relief for working class families? Alas, it doesn't exist! In the queue, we present the papers that say we have been awarded two medals for 'motherhood'.[16] And what do you think, this doesn't even get you milk. They say: where does the certificate say that you've got the right to get things without waiting your turn, or to get more than the rations allow? We can only shrug our shoulders. It's true. There simply isn't any help anywhere for people like us with large families. We're supposed to pin our medals on our chests and let the children look at them instead of eating. What's the point of them?

Housing for large families is not allocated as it should be by law. If you get anything it's by bribes, or by accepting what everyone else has turned down. As a rule, large families are badly treated at school, at work, in daily life.

b. Medical services are poor, ambulances don't come, and the

110

doctors don't care about you. (In hospital you get poor nursing, poor medical treatment and poor food.) It's like in *The Government Inspector* — the good patient gets better by himself.[17]

c. There are no grants to pay for medicine, and sick leave certificates — but you can't live on words alone.

4. I do not agree with the restriction of individual liberties and civil rights.

a. We have freedom to preach atheism, but not to preach religion. There are no religious publications, books, journals, newspapers, or radio and television programmes. Churches and monasteries are closed down on any pretext, and building new ones is simply unheard of.

b. Our trade unions have been merged into one organisation subordinated to the Party and the Government, although there are different unions for dockers, fishermen, sailors, metal workers, etc. Each has its own interests and problems. The trade unions should defend the rights of the workers against the Party and Government. They should have the right of collective bargaining and of demanding wage increases, better working conditions and holidays. The members of the leading bodies of the trade unions should be elected by, and chosen by, the workers themselves and not by the Politburo. The trade unions and the Party should be independent of one another. There is a special need for this at the level of the local city trade union committees, where lists of acceptable candidates (their lackeys and drinking companions) are prepared by the Party and given to the local trade union; then the illusion is created that they were chosen by the trade union meeting.

5a. The same sort of elections without election takes place in higher bodies as well. There, at some Party meeting, some friend or lackey of the bosses will stand up and nominate his chief. He praises him and they place him on the list of candidates; they have only one candidate on the list, so there isn't anybody to choose from. And even if it happens that he's a good deputy (to the Soviet), the rights and powers he's given are too few to enable him to help the people.

b. Our citizens are denied the right to demonstrate, strike and protest in other ways. And complaints do not help —

c. Citizens who disagree are persecuted by the police, the KGB, and at work by the management. This is what happened to me. I was persecuted for my demands for a better standard of living and pay, so that we and our children would not have to go hungry, would not have to go naked and barefoot, so that it would be possible to pay for school and all sorts of other things. At work they won't even let me into a higher grade than the fifth;[18] they won't let my wife work as a cleaner at the dry dock; they won't give me a visa for a cruise abroad.[19] They call me, seriously and in jest, 'an enemy of the people' and an anti-Soviet element. Who says this? The management.

d. The rights of the national republics, and in particular the Ukraine, should be restored and expanded. Education, at a school and university level, should be in Ukrainian. Institutions should also conduct their business in Ukrainian. The republic should have the right to have its own nationals as officials in all walks of life.[20]

e. Stop persecuting Solzhenitsyn, Sakharov, Tverdokhlebov, Bukovsky, V.Moroz, N.A.Strokatova, Dzyuba and Karavansky. [21] Give them the right to appear at meetings and let the people decide if they are right or wrong.

Free all political prisoners in the Soviet Union.

Down with the censorship of our post and publications.

6a. Work out a constitution which will guarantee the freedom of the citizen and put an end to the activities of the KGB. Let them chase foreign spies rather than 'witch-hunting' dissident citizens.

b. Work out laws that really guarantee freedom of speech, press, elections, assembly, demonstrations and strikes.

c. A law allowing free emigration.

Only in such a democratic and flourishing country will we agree to live and raise our children.

*L.M.Sery*
Odessa, 14 November 1976

★  ★ **Document 3/soon after 7 February 1978**
Open Letter
to George Meany and American Workers

Good day, dear Mr George Meany! Good day, my brother workers in America! I, a worker from the Ukraine, the father of seven young children, a champion of workers' rights, Leonid Mikhailovich Sery, turn to you. I wrote to you before, but I don't know if you received my letter, so I'm writing to you again.

Mr Meany!

Allow me to give you a brief description of the life of the workers at our enterprise. I work as a turner in the Il'ichevsky fishing port. We repair whalers and fishing boats. I earn 180-200 roubles a month. There are lots of things wrong with my job. We work on a piece-rate system, on a rota. However, when we come to work, we aren't given our rotas, and we don't see them till the end of the month. Our work is technically crude; we often don't make parts out of the materials we're supposed to. Our lack of technology, mistakes in design and draughtsmanship, and the shortage of essential tools leads to shoddy results. We have no files, hammers, spanners or grinding stones. There aren't enough spare parts, the machine-tools aren't repaired on schedule. All the workers have to bring their own tools to work (and they're almost impossible to obtain); accidents are common, because our safety equipment is in a bad state of repair, and there aren't enough protective measures.

They're always revising our norms and making us work harder to earn less. Every year there's a meeting and a new collective agreement is drawn up. At the meeting we're presented with a so-called 'agreement', by which the quota for the plan is increased by several per cent, while wages stay the same (that's what I'd call a one-sided agreement).

The workers' social services are badly organised. The majority of workers go to work without any breakfast and don't get anything to eat until dinner-time. The canteen's a long way away. There's no drinking water in the depot. Our dinner is badly cooked and costs a lot. You have to pay 70 kopeks-1 rouble for dinner and you're still hungry. There's a works bus to and from work (that is, there's supposed to be, but it doesn't always come), but we pay 4.50 roubles a quarter for it. At the moment, a turner's pay averages 200 roubles a month. As a result lots of workers see no reason to work hard and some even drink vodka at work. This has a lot to do with the inadequacies I've mentioned. But it's not just at work that things are bad.

For example, the price rises in the shops and the market, the shortages of food and basic necessities. Many workers, especially those with lots of children, don't see meat, butter, even borshch for months, not to mention fruit, vegetables and other vitamin foods.

They dress badly. Any one item costs all their pay, or at least half of it (a coat, a suit, shoes, etc.). In general, they don't live, but simply suffer, like me and my family. Who is it who is hit worst of all by the high prices and shortages if not workers and employees with big families. Couples with lots of children and single mothers are forced to have a savings account — if you don't have one, they don't give you your child allowance (four or seven roubles, depending on how many children you've got). Many people are also short of somewhere to live. There are people who wait dozens of years for a flat. People live where they can, in other people's flats, in pitiful hovels (cellars, attics and tumbledown sheds), which by your standards couldn't even be called slums.

Many families break up under the strain of such a life (the husband and wife get divorced), each of them quite justly finds fault with the other, they're sure that one of them must be to blame for the fact that they've no flat, no money, etc. They begin to drink to get away from it all.

But there are also some workers and employees who refuse to put up with this situation. They write to newspapers and magazines, to trade unions and even to the government. Some have hopes of getting justice and decent treatment, others have no such hope, and write simply to let people know what is going on, or even to 'put the finger on' who is to blame — the government, which has reduced the country to such a terrible state of poverty and injustice (although while they're doing this, they don't neglect themselves, they don't do so badly, they have everything you can think of and even more; all we get are promises of a golden future).

But they don't answer letters. Instead some people are persecuted for writing letters by the administrative organs, the police and the KGB. So it was and is with all who dare to criticise the way we live. So it was and is with me. I wrote lots of letters, full of all sorts of criticisms and suggestions but no-one bothered to reply to them.

If I called on the workers to work harder (and to tighten their belts), then they'd like it and even print what I wrote. But I wrote about the bad pay, the high prices, the unavailability of many goods, the thieving and bribery that goes on. I wrote about the poor medical services and the poor education that we get. I wrote about our trade unions, which have long since ceased to defend the workers and about the persecution of individuals and even peoples.

That men are persecuted for their convictions, I know from what's happened to me on more than one occasion. I have often (six times) been dragged to the KGB and the police station for questioning. They won't let me go on a mediterranean cruise ... And on 3 November 1977, I received a written threat from the KGB, saying that I was going to be tried, put in prison and then exiled for five years. I can't be put in prison — I'm the only breadwinner in the family. I've got a wife and seven children totally dependent on me ...

Recently a group of workers led by Vladimir Klebanov decided to form a trade union which would really defend the workers' rights. But the authorities are doing everything they can to stop them, and keep throwing their leaders in jail. That's what rights we've got. Your family starves — just you shut up about it; you're made to work for nothing — don't you complain; you're forced to work overtime — just you be pleased about it: or otherwise you'll be put behind bars. Our intelligentsia may not be allowed freedom of creativity, freedom of thought or speech, but it's far worse for the workers — they don't have the freedom to work, to eat, to rest, to strike or to form their own trade unions. Don't tell me this isn't slavery!

I beg you, tell your workers about this, and please give them a permit to go on holiday to the USSR, so that they can see for themselves the subject under discussion, and talk to the workers without the leadership being present. Our situation is very bad — poverty, hunger and lawlessness. In view of this, I am asking the government to allow me to emigrate, I can't stand living here any longer, and it wouldn't be fair for me to allow myself to be put in prison. I beg you, Mr Meany, defend our persecuted workers led by V.Klebanov, and help me and my family to leave the USSR. Goodbye dear friends.

L.Sery
Odessa


★ Document 4
To the All-Union Central Council of Trade Unions
From Leonid Mikhailovich Sery, worker
Declaration
Copies to:

115

Base Committee of the Ch. RPO Trade Union
'Antarctica'
Odessa Town Committee, BTOF

I, L.M.Sery, a lathe operator, have been a union member since 1952. I have worked in the above enterprise for eight years. I decided to leave the union for the following reasons:

1. The inability of this trade union to fight for workers' rights. (There is no right to demand, rather than to ask for, wage rises, price reductions, an improvement in work and leisure conditions).

2. The vassal-like subjection of the trade union to the authorities, the state and management. The management and the party bureau appoint the local committees, and dictate their terms to them. Workers' meetings are a mere formality.

3. Trade unions are unable to offer badly-off families the sort of help represented by 50 roubles per head, but it is impossible for these families to earn such a sum.[22]

4. The trade unions do not even defend us legally. And so we have to put up with calculated insults from a number of unscrupulous managers and workers. For example: 'Why have you produced so many children?', 'Wasn't there any light in your house?', and so on.

5. We get poor medical treatment. Our doctors do not carry out their duties conscientiously.

6. The same is true of schoolteachers. They call our children beggars and forbid the other children to make friends with them.

7. Ever since we were given a new flat we have suffered from cold, discomfort and its state of disrepair. Repairs to the flat have been dragging on since January. They send us wankers, not real workers.

All the things listed above make us think that we're not wanted. Therefore, the best way out of this situation is to leave the union in protest.

The father of many children
*Leonid M.Sery*
Worker
Odessa 27005, ul. Frunze 199, flat 128

# 5:

## Solidarity
### Introduction

The significance of the following document lies in the fact that it represents an attempt by dissident Soviet intellectuals to address the workers' movement in the West. It was signed by 85 supporters of the Russian, Lithuanian, and Ukrainian Helsinki monitoring groups campaigning for the implementation of the human rights section of the Helsinki Accords of 1975.

The background to the document is the systematic attempt by the Soviet regime to destroy the Helsinki groups, with heavy gaol-sentences being handed out to leading members of the groups (see note 2 below).

The dissidents' appeal to French workers to oppose the persecution of the civil rights campaigners initially fell on deaf ears. Communist and Socialist trade union officials blocked an attempt by Leonid Plyushch, the exiled Ukrainian marxist, to address workers at the Renault-Billancourt plant.

However, following the defeat of the Left in the general election of March 1978, the French Communist Party changed tack. Socialist and Communist trade unions participated in a press conference with Soviet and East European dissidents on 18 April 1978 and the CP supported a protest demonstration against the trials of Ginzburg and Shcharansky in July 1978.

Many socialists in the West justify their failure to support Soviet dissidents on the grounds of the latter's middle-class origins and right-wing politics. However, the position of Soviet *workers* — low living standards, absence of trade union organisation — is inseparable from the nature of the political regime in the USSR. The struggle for basic democratic freedoms is of as much interest to Soviet workers as it is to Soviet intellectuals.

Moreover, as the Czech Marxist Petr Uhl put it:
'*The* demands themselves *for democratic freedoms and civil rights*

117

*which cannot be realised under dictatorships can arouse the working class and other important layers of the working population, can heighten their fighting power, and shake the very foundations of the dictatorship ...*

*'The pro-capitalist illusions and reactionary myths that may guide this struggle initially weaken to the extent that the self-consciousness and self-confidence of the working class are raised.'*[1]

It is, therefore, essential that the workers' movement in the West should give its support to *all* those fighting for human rights in the Soviet Union and Eastern Europe.

★ **Document / 7 April 1977**
Appeal
to the Workers of the Renault Factories in France

On 2 March *Pravda* quoted Mark Ouin, General Manager of the Renault factories: 'Today Soviet orders represent approximately a quarter of our total machine-tool production'. The strengthening of economic and cultural ties between our countries means that people in one country cannot remain indifferent to what goes on in the other. We attach great importance to the views of workers throughout the world and on the political positions they take on international questions. We know that the Soviet leadership attaches equal importance to expressions of working class opinion. We would therefore like to make the following appeal to you:

Recently six members of the group monitoring the Helsinki Accords have been arrested — A.Ginzburg, Yu.Orlov, and A.Shcharansky (in Moscow), M.Rudenko and O.Tikhy (in the Ukraine), and Z.Gamsakhurdiya (in Georgia) as well as M. Kostava, a member of the Initiative Group for Human Rights in Georgia.[2] The activity of these groups consists of collecting and making public information about the way in which the human rights clauses of Helsinki are being implemented in the Soviet Union. However, those arrested find themselves accused of particularly serious state crimes and of slandering the social and

118

political regime. They face the threat of unjust condemnation to long and harsh terms of imprisonment.

The human rights clauses of the Helsinki Agreement play an extremely important role in the development of detente and the strenghtening of cooperation beween peoples. The fate of the arrested members of the 'Helsinki' groups is inseparable from these problems.

Bearing this in mind, and appealing to your sense of justice, we call on you not to rely solely on the Soviet or Western press in reaching your opinion on the matter, but to form a representative workers' committee empowered:

1. To study the basic information available on the work of these groups, and, in particular, to familiarise themselves with the documents which they sent to the governments of a number of countries which participated in the Helsinki Conference.

2. To study the information available on the arrest of the above members of these groups.

3. To send representatives to the Soviet Union to attend their trial or trials.

We are appealing through you to the whole of the French working class and we ask you to treat the case of the arrested members of the Helsinki group with all the seriousness demanded by the problem of human rights and international security.

Sincerely

[*Signed by eighty-five Soviet citizens*]

# Notes:
## General Introduction

[1] T.Cliff, *State Capitalism in Russia* (3rd ed.), London: Pluto Press 1974, pp.19-20.

[2] Miklos Haraszti, *A Worker in a Workers' State* (trans. M.Wright), Harmondsworth: Penguin 1977, pp.66, 40, 59.

[3] *ibid.* pp.99, 101

[4] Hedrick Smith, *The Russians* (2nd ed.), London: Sphere Books 1977, pp.266-7.

[5] A.Marchenko, *Arkhiv Samizdat* Document No.3197. (All following references to Marchenko are from this document.) Anatoly Marchenko received his first sentence (for having taken part in a brawl) — eight years, later commuted to two in 1958. He was then 20 and was working as a drilling foreman in Kaluga. Since then his history has been a string of convictions, trials, attempts to emigrate, etc. He is famous for his book *My Testimony* — memoirs of a labour camp. A self-educated worker who has chosen to side with the dissident intellectuals, he was sentenced to four years exile in Chuna in 1975.

[6] *Zhenshchini v SSSR*, Moscow 1975. (Official Soviet Statistics on Women.)

[7] A.E.Kotlyar and Ya.Turchkanova, *Zanyatost Zhenshchin v Proizvodstve* Moscow, 1975, p.23. (and *Zhenschchini v SSSR., op. cit.*)

[8] *ibid.* p.67.

[9] A.G.Kharchev and S.I.Golod, *Professional'naya Rabota Zhenshchin*, Leningrad 1971, p.70.

[10] *Zhenshchini v SSSR, op. cit.*

[11] D.Lane, *Politics and Society in the USSR* (2nd ed.), London: Martin Robertson 1978, p.399 (quoted from *Pravda* and *Narkhoz*).

[12] A.P.Volkov and others, *Trud i zarabotnaya plata v SSSR*, Moscow, 1968, (quoted in M. Mathews, *Class and Society in Soviet Russia,* London: Allen Lane, 1972, pp.82-90.)

[13] Lane, *op. cit.* p.292.

[14] G.E.Schroeder and B.S.Severin, 'Soviet consumption and incomes policies in perspective', in *Soviet Economy in a New Perspective*, Joint Economic Committee, US Congress, Washington 1976, p.623.

[15] Kotlyar, *op. cit.* p.14.

[16] Kharchev and Golod, *op. cit.* p.76. This seems to be the only Soviet survey which counts the number of appliances possessed by the working class as opposed to other sections of the population. The figures for Kostroma are higher because it's a slightly later survey, and an industrial town with more industrial goods available. The figures will be slightly higher now, since these were published in 1971.

[17] *ibid.* pp.83-85.

[18] K.Zukov and V.Fyodorov, *Housing Conditions in the Soviet Union*

(trans. V.S.Shcharkovich), Moscow: Progress Publishers 1974, Preface.

[19] Henry W. Morton, 'The Soviet urban scene', *Problems of Communism*, Jan-Feb 1977, p.76.

[20] A.D.Sakharov, *My Country and the World* (trans. G.V.Daniels), London: Collins, 1975, p.17.

[21] Zukov and Fyodorov, *op. cit.* p.19.

[22] Gregory Grossman, 'The "second" economy of the USSR', *Problems of Communism*, Sept-Oct 1977, p.26.

[23] Sakharov, *op. cit.* pp.21-3.

[24] *Zhenshchini v SSSR, op. cit.*

[25] G. Osipov, *Rabochi Klass i tekhnicheski progress*, Moscow 1965.

[26] Lane, *op. cit.* p.505.

[27] Isaac Deutscher, *Soviet Trade Unions*, London: Oxford University Press 1950, p.127.

[28] Collective Agreement 1975, for the 'Zaprozhstal' Iron and Steel Plant. Quoted in M. Costello, *Workers' Participation in the Soviet Union*, Moscow: Novosti Press Agency 1977, p.17.

[29] Deutscher, *op. cit.* pp.135-6. See David Lane for a more recent but almost identical account.

[30] Hedrick Smith, *op. cit.* p.276.

[31] M. Holubenko, 'The Soviet working class: discontent and opposition', *Critique* No.4, Spring 1975, p.20.

## The Right to Organise

[1] Document 7 in the FTUA Collection in our possession (see note 11 below): 'A Collective Complaint', 7 November 1977. If there are no specific references, quotations in this introduction come from documents printed here.

[2] Ever since Krushchev officially stressed 'the links between the Party and the People', the right to petition the highest authorities had been brought into prominence. See, for example, section 2 of the Rules of the Communist Party of the Soviet Union (*Ustav Kommunisticheskoi Sovetskovo Soyuza*, Moscow 1970, p.5): 'members of the Party ... must respond promptly to the enquiries and the needs of the working people'.

[3] FTUA Document 11 (see below).

[4] FTUA Document 15 (see below).

[5] A statement released to Agence France Presse in Moscow. Quoted in *Rouge*, 2 July 1978.

[6] *The Observer*, 2 July 1978.

[7] *Rouge*, 19 April 1978, and *Labour Focus on Eastern Europe*, May-June 1978.

[8] *The Observer*, 2 July 1978.

[9] See *Labour Focus*, May-June 1978.

[10]  *Trud* (the official paper of the Soviet trade unions), 11 June 1978. On 21 June 1978 the Head of the International Department of the All-Union Central Council of Trade Unions, V.E.Mozhayev, replied to a protest from the National Union of Railwaymen on behalf of the members of the Free Trade Union Association. He wrote 'We regret that a number of trade unions in Great Britain have been misled by propaganda inventions which have nothing to do with reality'.

[11]  The following documents of the Free Trade Union Association have reached the West:

1. Open letter (to International Opinion), 20 May 1977.
2. Letter from the Procurator's Office of the Baumansk District of Moscow to V.A.Klebanov, 17 June 1977.
3. Letter from the Procurator's Office of the USSR to V.A. Klebanov, 8 August 1977.
4. Letter from the Procurator's Office of the City of Moscow to V.A.Klebanov, 12 September 1977.
5. Open letter to International Opinion on the true situation of workers and employees on the eve of the 60th anniversary of the USSR, 19 September 1977.
6. Letter from the Secretary of the Moscow Region Trade Union Council to V.T.Poplavsky, 31 October 1977.
7. Collective complaint (to the leadership of the CPSU) demanding 'creation of an authoritative commission to investigate the activities of the Department of Administrative Organs of the Central Committee of the CPSU' and an audience with the leaders of the party and government, 7 November 1977.
8. Letter from the Editorial Board of *Izvestia* to V.V.Chetverikova, 8 December 1977.
9. Letter from the Editorial Board of *Izvestia* to V.T.Poplavsky, 8 December 1977.
10. Letter from the Ministry of Internal Affairs to V.I.Kucherenko, 16 December 1977.
11. Appeal to Yu.V.Andropov, Chairman of the KGB, demanding the release of V.A.Klebanov from Moscow Psychiatric Hospital No.7, 21 December 1977.
12. Letter from the Procurator's Office of the USSR to V.I. Kucherenko, 26 December 1977.
13. Letter from the Editorial Board of *Izvestia* to V.F.Luchkov, 2 January 1978.
14. Letter to Yu.V.Andropov demanding the release of G.T.Yankov from Moscow Psychiatria Hospital No.3, 12 January 1978.
15. Letter to Yu.V.Andropov protesting against treatment of P.F. Reznichenko, Klebanov, Yankov and other members of the group, 27 January 1978.
16. Appeal to International Opinion (a shortened version of No.15), 28 January 1978.
17. Open letter to Soviet non-governmental organisations, to Party and Soviet bodies, to the national press and journals of the USSR, 30 January 1978.

18. Open letter to correspondents of the Western press agencies accredited in the USSR, 1 February 1978.
19. Appeal to the ILO and to trade unions in the West, 1 February 1978.
20. Copy of the ILO's Convention 87 — guaranteeing freedom of association and the right to organise, 1 February 1978.
21. Statute of the Free Trade Union Association of the Soviet Working People, 1 February 1978.
22. List of 110 candidate members, 1 February 1978.
23. Klebanov's autobiography 1958-75 (very badly produced) no date.

[12] a. Party cards were recalled and reissued in 1972. Lenin (Vladimir Ilyich) did it in 1921.
   b. Internal passports are being issued to *all* citizens. Until now workers on collective farms had no passports and were thus tied to the land. They'll all have them by 1982. This is largely legal recognition of the fact that collective farm workers were flocking to the towns legally or illegally.

[13] *Izvestia* — 'News', daily paper of the Supreme Soviet.
   *Pravda* — 'Truth', daily paper of the Communist Party of the Soviet Union.
   *Trud* — 'Labour', the official Soviet trade union newspaper.
   *Literaturnaya Gazeta* — 'Literary Gazette', the weekly newspaper of the Writers' Union.
   *Ogonyok* — 'Little Flame', a popular illustrated weekly.
   *Kommunist* — the Party journal.
   *Partinaya Zhizn* — 'Party Life', a bi-weekly Party paper.
   *Sotsialisticheskaya Zakonnost* — 'Socialist Legality', the publication of the Ministry of Justice.

[14] *Leninskoye Znamya* — 'Leninist Banner', the provincial newspaper for towns around Moscow.

[15] Every town has its drunk tanks or 'trezviteli', usually very over-crowded. Habitual offenders have their head shaved.

[16] 'While in Germany between 1967 and 1972 about 5% of the work-force changed their jobs each year and an equal amount in the USA (4.8%, 2.1% at their own request), the comparable figure for the USSR was 21% in 1970', W.Teckenberg, 'Labour turnover and job satisfaction: indicators of industrial conflict in the USSR?', *Soviet Studies*, April 1978, no.2, p.194.

[17] *Vechernaya Moskva* — 'Evening Moscow', the daily evening paper.

[18] The account of the period 1958-75 is based on the autobiography (FTUA Document 23), the later history on other documents in the collection.

[19] Article 187-1 of the Ukrainian Criminal Code is the same as article 190-1 of the Criminal Code of the RSFSR — slandering the Soviet state, see note on Ivanov for the text of the Russian code.

[20] On 8 January 1977 a bomb went off in a train in the Moscow Metro, killing at least four people. Dissident sources suggest that it was the work of three Armenians who belonged to a group advocating the

separation of Armenia from the Soviet Union. However, Sakharov expressed the fear that it was a KGB plot to incriminate dissidents and the KGB have certainly been using it that way. Klebanov and other members of his group, and Rubtsov, a friend of Sakharov's are only a few of the people who have been arrested on this pretext. And they're still arresting people — on 7 June 1978 Tass announced that yet more bombers had been caught!

[21] Amnesty International press release, 1 May 1978.

[22] These case histories have been compiled from the (very repetitive) information given in Documents 1, 5, 7 and 17 of the Free Trade Union Association. All statements in the first person are from Document 5.

[23] An entire wing of the Rossiya, a gigantic modern hotel in Red Square, burnt down on 25 February 1977, probably due to an electrical fault. Six people died, 12 were injured.

[24] All the information on Gaidar is from an Amnesty International press release 1 March 1978.

[25] i.e., in a lower-skilled grade (though still quite a high one).

[26] Each Soviet enterprise is organised rather like an army. The enterprise is divided into shops, the shops into brigades. Each brigade has its 'brigade leader', a sort of sergeant in charge.

[27] Russian families, usually those who are trying to emigrate, often try to rush past the KGB into the American embassy in Moscow, under the completely mistaken impression that the US government has the right to grant them asylum. They are always beaten up, imprisoned, etc., by the KGB afterwards.

[28] The information about Nikolayev's earlier history comes from a biography of him issued by Amnesty International in April 1978. This includes an account of a conversation with his psychiatrist also published in the *Chronicle of Human Rights in the USSR*, New York, No.11-12, September-December 1974.

[29] An individual can travel abroad only if s/he has a personal invitation from someone in the country s/he wishes to visit *and* the Party's approval.

[30] As Solzhenitsyn says, 'Oh you citizens, you love to travel! Do not forget that in every station there are a GPU branch and several prison cells', *The Gulag Archipelago* I, (trans. T.P.Whitney) 5th ed., London: Collins-Fontana 1977, p.9.

[31] Document Nos. 15 and 16 in our FTUA collection. (see note 11).

[32] He lives with his son on this amount, though the legal minimum income is 50 roubles per head.


## The Right to Strike

[1] M.Holubenko, 'The Soviet working class: discontent and opposition', *Critique*, No.4, Spring 1975, p.17. This extremely important article is the main source for this introduction.

[2] Vadim Belotserkovsky, an unpublished interview with Valentin Ivanov, broadcast on Radio Liberty at the beginning of 1978.

[3] Cornelia Gerstenmaier, *Voices of the Silent*, New York 1972. Quoted in M.Holubenko, *op. cit.*, pp.13-14.

[4] *An Interview with Leonid Plyushch*, Toronto: Diyaloh, p.12. The interview took place in France on 12 February 1976.

[5] There are details of these events in 'Rabochie Vystuplenia v SSSR v machale 60kh godov', a chapter of a forthcoming book by Vadim Belotserkovsky.

[6] M.Holubenko, *op. cit.* p.9.

[7] *Labour Focus on Eastern Europe*, May-June 1978.

[8] Reported in *A Chronicle of Current Events*, the clandestine journal of the intellectual opposition. It's the only industrial action they've mentioned.

[9] This document has now found its way to the *Archiv Samizdat* — No. 3046. A translation of it has also been published in *Socialist Challenge*, 8 June 1978.

[10] John Kolasky, *Two Years in Soviet Ukraine*, Toronto: Peter Martin Associates 1972, pp.191-2.

[11] A.I.Solzhenitsyn, *The Gulag Archipelago*, III, (trans. H.T. Willetts), London: Collins and Harvill Press 1978, pp.507-14.

[12] This document was published in a pamphlet written by Andrea Martin, *Ukraine — Unrest and Repression*, London: Committee to Defend Ivan Dzyuba and Vyacheslav Chornovil, 1973. The editors are grateful to Andrea Martin for allowing them to use this document. It was also published with an introduction giving additional information in Ted Harding, 'Kiev workers protest to the Central Committee', *Critique*, No.2.

[13] Colonel Lavrenchuk — deputy head of the regional administration of the Ministry of the Interior and member of the regional Party organisation.

[14] Internal passports are issued with considerable discrimination. One reason for this is that by denying internal passports for workers, managers have a hold on the labour force no matter how dissatisfied the workers might be with the wages, housing and working conditions.

## The Right to Protest

[1] 'Declaration' by Bogolyubov about the way the Magadan KGB have been persecuting him for his views. November 1976.

[2] V.V.Opukiyenko and V.A.Popovkin, *Kompletnoye Issledovaniye Migrasiyonnikh Prosessov*, Moscow: Statistika 1973.

[3] *Itogi Vsesoyuznoi Perepisi Naseleniya — 1970*, IV, Moscow:

Statistika 1973, pp.152-191; *Ukraina v Tsifrakh — 1927*, Kharkov 1927, p.11.

[4] Article 62-1 of the Ukrainian Criminal Code is the same as article 70 of the Criminal Code of the RSFSR — 'agitation or propaganda carried out for the purpose of subverting or undermining the Soviet regime'.

[5] Harry Bridges is the long-standing leader of the International Longshoremen's and Warehousemen's Union (ILWU), based on the west coast of the United States. The ILWU is a traditional stronghold of the violently pro-Moscow Communist Party of the USA.

[6] Article 206 refers to 'hooliganism', 'deliberate actions which grossly violate the social order and express grave disrespect towards society' (*Ugolovny Kodeks RSFSR*, Moscow: Yuridicheskaya Literatura, 1970, p.78).

[7] Article 197 provides a maximum penalty of six months' imprisonment or hard labour or a fine of 50 roubles for 'violations of the rules of entry, residence or registration in the border or border zone' (*Ugolovny Kodeks, op. cit.* p.74).

[8] See note 11 to The Right to Emigrate.

[9] Savva Morozov was one of the first examples of the rich serf manufacturer. He founded one of the first large textile factories in Russia at the beginning of the 19th century. In 1820 he bought his freedom for 17,000 roubles from his owner Riumin.

[10] Article 224 is the section on drugs offences (*Ugolovny Kodeks, op. cit.* p.85).

[11] On Meany see note 10 to The Right to Emigrate.

[12] FZO, Faculty of Extra-Mural Studies.

[13] He'd been working as a teacher. In February 1967 he was arrested. In April he was sentenced to three years' imprisonment and barred from teaching for five years supposedly for 'slandering the Soviet regime' and 'educating youth in a nationalist spirit'.

[14] The first agreement between Russia and the Urkaine was the Treaty of Pereiaslav in 1654. The Hetman (supreme leader of the Cossacks) Bohdan Khmelnytsky 'accepted the protection of the Muscovite Tsar, but still remain a separate body politic', *Ukraine — Concise Encyclopaedia*, I, University of Toronto Press (Canada) 1963, p.64.

[15] Khmelnytsky was Hetman of the Ukrainian Cossacks from 1648 to 1657.

[16] Oleksander Ivanovich Oles (1878-1944), an outstanding Ukrainian poet, emigrated after the revolution. He was not published in the USSR between 1931 and 1957. This book, *Tvori*, was published in Kiev in 1971, not in 1970 as Rebryk says.

*The Right to Emigrate*

[1] From the Helsinki monitoring group's introduction to their

'Document 1 on emigration'.

[2] Some of the documents say six — his seventh child, Diana, was born on 9 April 1977.

[3] Committee for the Defense of Soviet Political Prisoners, press release, New York, 20 April 1978.

[4] Druzhinniki — People's Auxiliary Policemen, officially said to number 7 million in 1971. F.S. Razarenov ed., *Narodnomu Druzhinniku*, Moscow: Znaniya 1973, p.115.

[5] Vladimir Belotserkovsky, unpublished interview with Valentin Ivanov, broadcast on Radio Liberty at the beginning of 1978 (this took place in Italy soon after Ivanov left the USSR).

[6] A document compiled by five members of the Helsinki monitoring group — Lyudmila Alekseyeva, Aleksandr Ginzburg, Melva Landa, Yuri Orlov, Anatoly Shcharansky. We have re-ordered the material for editorial convenience.

[7] This is a reference to the so-called 'communist' Saturdays and Sundays when everyone works without pay. They are universally known as 'black' Saturdays and Sundays.

[8] UMZ, Prison Administration.

[9] George Meany, President of the American Federation of Labour-Congress of Industrial Organisation (AFL—CIO) is a favourite target of appeals from persecuted Soviet workers. Ironically, he is the living symbol of the right-wing leadership of the American labour movement, which collaborates very closely with the employers and the state and is bitterly opposed to rank-and-file control of the trade unions. He also has long-standing links with the CIA.

[10] Article 190-1 is the statute usually used against oppositionists. It states: 'For the systematic spreading in an oral form, of slanders against the Soviet state and society — and equally the fabrication or spreading of such slanders in written, printed or other form — the penalty is imprisonment for up to 3 years, or one year's hard labour, or a fine of 100 roubles'.

[11] Two separate hijackings of planes to Turkey took place in 1970. The first was by two Soviet students, who hijacked a five-seater plane and were later given stiff prison sentences by a Soviet court. The same year, a Lithuanian father and son hijacked another plane from the Soviet Union to Turkey. The two were sentenced to terms in a Turkish prison, were later granted an amnesty, and then travelled to South America and the United States. (*The Guardian*, 27 May 1977).

[12] Angela Davis, a leading black member of the Communist Party of the USA, was charged with conspiracy to murder for allegedly supplying some of the weapons used in an unsuccessful attempt to free George Jackson and the other Soledad Brothers in 1970. After a prolonged manhunt she was captured by the FBI and put on trial. After an international campaign in which the Communist Parties played a prominent role, she was acquitted in 1972.

[13] *Za Rubezhom* — 'Abroad', digest of international news.

[14] The Germans occupied the Ukraine from 1941-44. During this

period any Communist Party members they could find, they killed. The driver Afanas'yev is presumably a reference to some recent event.

[15] There are approximately half a million Ukrainians in Canada; Toronto alone has a Ukrainian population of 50,000.

[16] Motherhood medals were introduced in 1944 to encourage people to have large families. The first class is awarded to women with six children, the second to those with seven. Sery's wife Valentina had a seventh child, Diana, in April 1977, so she now qualifies for the medal of Motherhood Glory second class. Women with ten or more children become 'heroine mothers'.

[17] The reference is to Gogol's play *The Government Inspector*. In it, Strawberry, the warden of the local hospital, says of his patients: 'There aren't more than ten of them left. The rest have all recovered. We've got it all arranged that way now, it's our method. You may find this hard to believe, but since I took charge they've all been recovering like flies. A patient is hardly admitted to the Infirmary before he recovers, and not so much through drugs as through conscientiousness and method'. *Four Russian Plays* (trans. J.Cooper), Harmondsworth: Penguin 1972, p.260.

[18] 'All trades in the Soviet Union are broken down into grades or razryady. There are four sets or scales of razryady in industry, and three in construction, each scale being composed of between six and ten razryady'. There are also scales of working ability, kvalifikatsii, which correspond to the razryady. The worker is supposed to apply to the management when he thinks he is competent to be moved into a higher razryad. See M.Matthews, *Class and Society in Soviet Russia*, London: Allen Lane, 1972, p.111.

[19] Sery seems to feel very aggrieved about this. He's talking about a trip round the Mediterranean on one of the Soviet ships that run from Odessa. These trips are a safe way of rewarding local officials etc. for good behaviour — they get a glimpse of the West while remaining firmly attached to Soviet territory.

[20] Ukrainians have to speak Russian in school; Ukrainian only appears as one of the foreign language options on the syllabus. See Rebryk (pp.95-97) for more about Ukrainian nationalism.

[21] Alexander Solzhenitsyn was deported from the USSR in 1974; Andrey Sakharov and Andrey Tverdokhlebov are both leading human rights activists in Moscow — Tverdokhlebov was arrested in 1975; Vladimir Bukovsky was freed and deported to the West in 1976, in exchange for Luis Corvolan, leader of the Chilean Communist Party; Valentyn Moroz is serving a nine-year sentence for anti-Soviet agitation; Ivan Dzyuba, author of a celebrated marxist attack on the oppression of non-Russian nationalities in the USSR, *Internationalism or Russification* (1968), was arrested in 1972 and has since become an apologist for the regime (see his 'self-criticism', *Facets of a Crystal*, 1976); Svyatoslav Karavansky has been in and out of Soviet prisons since 1944; his wife, Nina Strokatova, after

serving a sentence in the Morodovian labour camps, is now in internal exile; Moroz, Dzyuba, Karavansky and Strokatova all come from the Ukraine.

[22] Soviet sociologists regard a monthly income of 50 roubles per head as the minimum standard of living.


## Solidarity

[1] *Labour Focus on Eastern Europe*, May-June 1977.
[2] Alexander Ginzburg has been sentenced to eight years' in a labour camp (July 1978) and Yuri Orlov to seven years' imprisonment and five years' penal exile for 'anti-Soviet agitation and propaganda' (May 1978); Anatoly Shcharansky to 13 years' prison and labour camp for 'espionage' and 'anti-Soviet agitation' (July 1978); Mykola Rudenko and Oleksa Tikhy to 12 and 15 years' respectively (June 1977); Zviad Gamsakhurdia and Merab Kostava to five years each (May 1978).